Fleeing for Freedom

LIBERTY LINE.
NEW ARRANGEMENT---NIGHT AND DAY.

The improved and splendid Locomotives, Clarkson and Lundy, with their trains fitted up in the best style of accommodation for passengers, will run their regular trips during the present season, between the borders of the Patriarchal Dominion and Libertyville, Upper Canada. Gentlemen and Ladies, who may wish to improve their health or circumstances, by a northern tour; are respectfully invited to give us their patronage:

SEATS FREE, *irrespective of color*.

Necessary Clothing furnished gratuitously to such as have *"fallen among thieves."*

"Hide the outcasts—let the oppressed go free."—*Bible*.

☞For seats apply at any of the trap doors, or to the conductor of the train.

J. CROSS, *Proprietor*.

N. B. For the special benefit of Pro-Slavery Police Officers, an extra heavy wagon for Texas, will be furnished, whenever it may be necessary, in which they will be forwarded as dead freight, to the "Valley of Rascals," always at the risk of the owners.

☞Extra Overcoats provided for such of them as are afflicted with protracted *chilly-phobia*.

Fleeing for Freedom

Stories of the Underground Railroad
As Told by Levi Coffin and William Still

Edited with an Introduction by
GEORGE AND WILLENE HENDRICK

CHICAGO
Ivan R. Dee

Library of Congress Cataloging-in-Publication Data:
Fleeing for freedom : stories of the Underground Railroad / as told by Levi Coffin and William Still ; edited with an introduction by George and Willene Hendrick.
    p. cm.
    Includes bibliographical references (p.) and index.
    Contents: Selections from Levi Coffin's Reminiscences — Selections from William Still's The Underground Rail Road.
    ISBN 1-56663-545-4 (acid-free paper) — ISBN 1-56663-546-2 (pbk. : acid-free paper)
    1. Coffin, Levi, 1798–1877. 2. Still, William, 1821–1902. 3. Underground railroad. 4. Underground railroad—Indiana. 5. Underground railroad—Ohio. 6. Fugitive slaves—United States—History—19th century. 7. Antislavery movements—Pennsylvania—Philadelphia—History—19th century. 8. Antislavery movements—United States—History—19th century. 9. Abolitionists—United States—Biography. 10. African American abolitionists—Biography. I. Coffin, Levi, 1798–1877. Reminiscences of Levi Coffin. Selections. II. Still, William, 1821–1902. Underground Railroad. Selections. III. Hendrick, George. IV. Hendrick, Willene, 1928–

E450.F535 2004
973.7'115—dc21

2003055071

For B. J. Bolden, Mark L. Collins, Casey Diana,
Katherine Karle, Douglas LaPrade, Fritz Oehlschlaeger,
David Rachels, Judy Rosenberg, Leonard A. Slade, Jr.

Contents

Preface

"OPPRESSED SLAVES should flee and take the Liberty Line to freedom." This was an important message of the 1844 *Western Citizen* drawing and accompanying text that is reproduced opposite the title page of this book. We begin this collection of Underground Railroad stories, related by Levi Coffin and William Still, with that sketch of an engine pulling four train cars filled with passengers and actually headed underground on its way to Canada. For seats on the train, fugitives were to apply to the Rev. John Cross of Illinois. This early image of the Underground Railroad is a literal representation of the mostly secret operation to transport fugitives to freedom. The text, undoubtedly by Cross, is filled with bitter humor.

Another prominent abolitionist who helped oppressed slaves is discussed in the Introduction because of his involvement in the escape of Eliza Harris, a major character in *Uncle Tom's Cabin*. He was the Rev. John Rankin, a Presbyterian minister from Ripley, Ohio, and a station master who often sent escaping slaves, including Eliza Harris, on to Levi Coffin. Rankin wrote this undramatic and unemotional account of the Underground Railroad as he knew it, accurate as far as it went but omitting the violence of the pro-slavery opponents and the dangers faced by escaping slaves and the conductors who helped them:

> I kept a depot on what was called the Underground railway. It was so called because they who took passage on it disappeared from public view as really as if they had gone into the ground. After the fugitive slaves entered a depot on that road, no trace of them could be found. They were secretly passed from one depot to another until they arrived in Canada. This road extended its branches through all the free

states. These were formed without any general concert. There was no secret society organized. There were no secret oaths taken, nor promises of secrecy extorted. And yet there were no betrayals. Anti-slavery persons were actuated by a sense of humanity and right, and, of course, were true to one another. It may seem incredible that lines over so extensive a region as that of the free states should have been formed without some general council having been held, but it is true that there was no such council. These lines were formed in the following manner. There were anti-slavery men living at various points on the border of the free states. With them fugitives would stop, and this made it necessary for safety to find some anti-slavery men on the way to whom these fugitives could be taken. I will give my own case as an instance. I lived on the top of a high hill at Ripley. The house was in full view of Kentucky. The slaves by some means discovered that I was an abolitionist, and consequently, when any of them ran away, they came to my house, and I knew that there were anti-slavery men on Red Oak, at Decatur, and Sardinia, and hence I could send them to any one of these places, and I had sons to convey them to such places as I chose to send them. And then they could be sent . . . from point to point until they arrived in Canada.

In our Introduction and in the texts by Levi Coffin and William Still, the hardships of slaves and the dangers the conductors faced are explored. Rankin's abolitionist activities have been too little known in the past century, but Ann Hagedorn in her excellent study *Beyond the River* (2003) has brought him to public attention once again. As one reviewer of Hagedorn's book has perceptively noted, "John Brown, Frederick Douglass, Rankin—the U.S. produced men like that because slavery, the nation's fatal flaw, was awful enough to breed opponents of equal fury." Rankin passionately fought for escaping slaves, but his written account of the Underground Railroad is bland and less dramatic than the stories by Coffin and Still.

In planning this collection, we debated the kinds of selections to be included. We admired Charles L. Blockson's *The Underground Railroad* (1987). He reproduced brief selections from well-known works by William and Ellen Craft, William Wells Brown, and Frederick Douglass but also used relatively unknown narratives by Philip Younger, Patrick Smead, Eber Pettit, and many others. Blockson's excellent approach need not be repeated here. Instead we decided to concentrate on two classic works—Levi Coffin's *Reminiscences* and William Still's *The Underground Rail Road.* Coffin was a Quaker who worked out of Indiana and Ohio; Still was a free black man who was secretary of the Philadelphia Vigilance Committee. Both wrote detailed accounts of their abolitionist activities and the slaves they aided. Their long books, each more than seven hundred pages, are now too little read, in part because of their daunting length. We have chosen representative stories from their works, which we hope will make them more readily available to a modern audience.

In the Introduction we trace the growth of the Underground Railroad movement in the United States, followed by biographical accounts of Coffin and Still.

The literature on the history of the Underground Railroad is extensive, and at the beginning of the Notes section we include an annotated bibliography of some of the most useful accounts.

In the nineteenth century, when Coffin and Still engaged in Underground Railroad activities, slavery was legal in the United States. Coffin, Still, and other abolitionists broke state and federal laws as they aided fugitive slaves attempting to gain their freedom. Escaping slaves were also breaking state and federal laws. Brave men, women, and children, black and white, worked together on the Liberty Line. Here are some of their most memorable stories.

Fleeing for Freedom

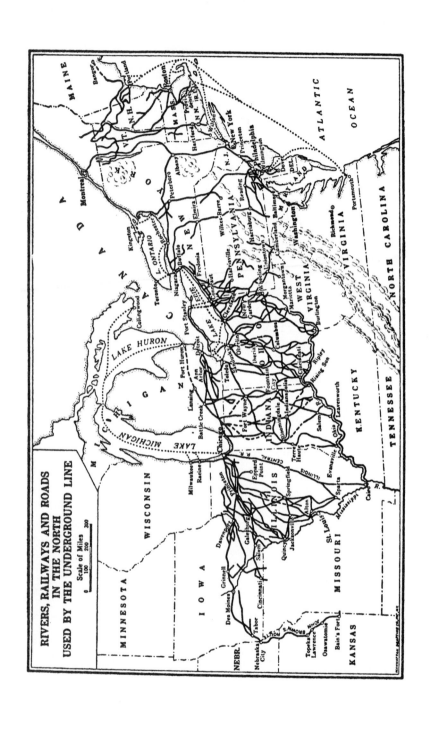

RIVERS, RAILWAYS AND ROADS
IN THE NORTH
USED BY THE UNDERGROUND LINE

Scale of Miles
0   100   200   300

Introduction

⊂≣ The Underground Railroad, which operated in the United States from late in the eighteenth century until the early years of the Civil War in the 1860s, was an informal, constantly changing network of routes over which fugitive slaves were passed along, often at night, from Border and Southern states to Canada or to a safe city in the North. Runaway slaves were helped in an organized way before 1830, but there was no widely recognized name for this activity. When trains were introduced into the United States in that year, the steam engine and the rail lines connecting cities and towns began to capture the American imagination, and those running the mostly secret operation for helping slaves escape began to adopt railroad terminology, using such terms as "passenger," "depot" or "station," "ticket agents," "station master," and "conductor."

The origin of the term "Underground Railroad" is enveloped in myth, but one often-repeated story involves a slave named Tice Davids who in 1831 ran away from Kentucky to Ohio. The escapee was closely followed by his master, and when Davids reached the river he jumped in and swam into Ripley, where there were several abolitionists. Davids's owner took some time to locate a skiff, and by the time he made it across the river Davids had disappeared. The Kentucky slave owner then thought "The nigger must have gone off on an underground road."

Larry Gara in *The Liberty Line* gives another account of the origin of the term. The Chicago *Western Citizen* for December 23, 1842, he writes, carried a story about a slave who escaped but then returned South. He was tortured and said "that the abolitionists had a *railroad under ground* and that he started for it; but when he got there the 'trap-door' was shut."

These stories are probably apocryphal, but conductors on this shadowy line did hide escaping slaves and transport them by buggy or wagon to the next station a few miles away. Conductors and escapees were in danger. The fugitive slave, if captured, would most often be returned to bondage. Arrested conductors were often subjected to heavy fines. The conductor and the passengers used great caution; once they approached the next station, the conductor had to alert that station master. Often the "hoot-owl" sound would be made and returned. At other times there were secret knocks on the door or window. And at times cryptic notes were sent ahead, such as this one by John Stone of Belpre, Ohio, to David Putnam, dated August 1843:

Business is arranged for Saturday night be on the lookout and if practicable let a carriage come & meet the cara*wan* J S

Slaves could also be hidden under bags of grain in farm wagons and moved during daylight hours. The stations were safe houses and typically had hiding places for the fugitives in cellars, attics, or barns. The house of Levi Coffin in Newport, Indiana, contained an indoor well allowing the Coffins to conceal the unusual amount of water needed for the runaways in hiding there.

Eventually the fugitive, unless captured, would reach Canada or a safe community such as New Bedford, Massachusetts. John Rankin and Levi Coffin describe the Midwestern, rural routes of the Liberty Line. Conductors working out of New York and Philadelphia, as the rail system expanded, put escaping slaves on above-ground trains, in some instances hidden in baggage cars by sympathetic conductors of real trains. Slaves also escaped on riverboats and domestic ocean-going vessels. In one story in this collection, an escaping slave rides to freedom on top of train cars.

Within a short time after slaves were brought to Jamestown, Virginia, in 1619, and then to other settlements, they began to escape, and slave owners began to call for official action to solve that problem. The New England Confederation of Plymouth, Massachusetts, Connecticut, and New Haven in 1643 agreed that there should be no harboring of slaves. That agreement had little effect, and the flights of slaves continued. Some took up life with Indians; others remained in areas of the colonies where there was anti-slavery sentiment. Before the American Revolution fugitive slaves could count on help from fellow blacks, from some Indian tribes, and from a few white men and women.

After the Declaration of Independence in 1776, with its stirring words about all men being created equal and about human freedom, more people in the colonies began to believe that these words should apply equally to blacks in slavery. One religious group in particular, the Society of Friends (Quakers), began to play a major role in the anti-slavery movement, to the distress of plantation owners. On May 12, 1786, George Washington wrote about a slave from Alexandria, Virginia, who had escaped to Philadelphia and "whom a society of Quakers in the city, formed for such purposes, have attempted to liberate." Washington was clearly unhappy about systematic efforts to help slaves. He wrote on November 20 the same year about one of his slaves whom he had sent to William Drayton and who had escaped: "The gentleman to whose care I sent him has promised every endeavor to apprehend him, but it is not easy to do this, when there are numbers who would rather facilitate the escape of slaves than apprehend them when runaways."

In Philadelphia in 1787 the sixteen- or seventeen-year-old Isaac T. Hopper, a Quaker, began his lifetime of work helping escaped slaves. He perfected his underground methods there and in 1829 moved to New York City where he continued his efforts.

Hopper was swift to act on behalf of fugitive slaves. Once, when informed that an escapee had been captured by his master and was soon to be moved south, Hopper rushed to the tavern where the slave was being held, bounded up the stairs, and was summarily thrown out the window by six guards. Although bruised, he raced again to the second-floor room, broke down the door, startled the guards, and freed the slave. He was an activist friend of the escaped slaves and often used the legal system to the slaves' advantage, tying up the owners in court for months.*

Quakers were not the only religious group aiding runaways. Unitarian, Wesleyan, Presbyterian, and other churches contained members whose consciences had led them to believe that slavery was wrong. Most organized religious groups in the South, however, defended the institution of slavery, declaring it was ordained by God. They quoted biblical verses to uphold that position. Significant numbers of Northern churches ignored the issue of slavery.

Although it is impossible to find an accurate accounting of the number of slaves who escaped from the colonies and later from slave-holding states, the numbers were significant. It has been estimated that from 1830 to 1860, 9,000 escapees passed through Philadelphia; Levi Coffin is said to have helped about 3,000. Rev. Rankin assisted about 2,000, but some of these passed through the Coffin station. A few helpers, such as the black woman Harriet Tubman, are well known for their work as conductors, but hundreds of little-known people, black and white, were involved in the effort. For their own safety, most did not publicize their work in freeing slaves. Just how many fugitives made it to Canada by the time of the Civil War is considered to be between 20,000 and 75,000, and, of course, many fugitive slaves remained in the Northern states. Some escapees became part of the gold rush in California; others went to the gold fields in Australia, and some sought safety in Britain.

As William Still, the black man who headed the Vigilance Committee in Philadelphia, wrote in *The Underground Rail Road,* the escapees came "from rice swamps and cotton fields . . . from kitchens

---

*Charles L. Blockson, in *The Underground Railroad,* argues, "The Quakers have long enjoyed the reputation of being the most active in the Underground Railroad. Various sources, however, belie this image; only a small minority of this small community raised their voices against slavery and participated in the struggles to transport slaves to freedom." Nonetheless Quakers such as Hopper and Coffin were among the most active conductors.

and mechanic shops, from Border States and Gulf States; from cruel masters and mild masters"—and, one should not forget, from mild mistresses and cruel mistresses. Many were aided by fellow slaves and free blacks whose names are now lost. Slaves who refused to continue in bondage and those who helped runaways in various ways knew that some fugitives walked for protection in the woods and fields at night, following the North Star. Others fled by sea or river, often after bribing captains or sailors for their help. These fugitive men, women, and children were frequently pursued by bloodhounds, posses, or "owners" intent upon capturing their "property." Some of the slaves disguised themselves—men as women, women as men—to escape their pursuers. Some with fair skin passed as white and took above-ground trains or ships to a hospitable state and then on to Canada. Some were armed and had no hesitation about using their weapons when confronted by armed patrols or posses. Some came with scarred backs from whippings; many came with scarred psyches from mistreatment during their years in slavery. Some had forged papers, supposedly signed by their masters, allowing them to travel. Some of the fugitives had first escaped to woods or swamps and lived in the rough for weeks or months before making their way northward. They arrived in tattered clothes, sometimes vermin infested. Most came without funds. Some came with gunshot wounds from patrollers or posse members. Some escaped because they feared being sold "down the river" to the New Orleans slave auctions, separated forever from spouses and children and condemned to the Deep South where the life expectancy for slaves was short. Others had the entrepreneurial spirit and hoped to work for themselves, not for an "owner." Whatever the reasons, these slaves were willing to risk their lives to gain their freedom.

And all these runaway slaves were deliberately disobeying state and federal laws. The Constitution of the United States, ratified in 1788, stated in Article 4, No. 2: "No person held to service or labor in one state under the laws thereof, escaping into another, shall, in consequence of any law or regulation therein, be discharged from such service or labor, but shall be delivered up on claim of the party to whom such service or labor may be due." But this section of the Constitution was generally not enforced, and slaves continued to flee, aided by those who opposed that peculiar institution. The runaways tended to settle in Northern states.

Congress in 1793 passed a Fugitive Slave Law which allowed slave owners or their agents to seize fugitives, take them before a federal or local judge, and claim that the blacks had escaped from their owner. The owner or the agent might then receive a warrant, permitting him to remove the runaways from the state or territory where they had been captured. The law provided for a $500 fine for harboring or hindering the arrest of an escaped slave.

Some arrests of fugitive slaves occurred under this law, and fines were levied against those who aided the runaways. Slave-holding states also passed laws forbidding the aiding and harboring of slaves, and these were more often applied than the federal law was. In either jurisdiction, the judgments could be harsh. The Quaker Thomas Garrett was convicted in Delaware in 1848 of aiding slave children. After he was convicted, most of his property was seized to pay his fine. Yet he was not broken in spirit; he told the judge: "[N]ow that thee hast relieved me of what little I possessed, I will go home and put another story on my house. I want room to accommodate more of God's poor."

Slave owners were angered by the activities of abolitionists, at times using mob violence against them. In 1838 they offered bounties of $500 to $2,500 for the abduction or assassination of the Rev. John Rankin, the Presbyterian minister in Ripley, Ohio, and several other abolitionists. Men and women of conscience were undeterred and went on helping fugitive slaves, and the exodus from the South continued. As Gara wrote in *The Liberty Line*, "The number of slaves who escaped from southern bondage was not large. The exact number, of course, can never be determined. The legend puts it high, but in actual fact the proportion of runaways to the entire slave population was small."

Black and white conductors helping fugitive slaves worked quietly and secretly because of the dangers posed by bounty hunters and by federal laws criminalizing their activities, but John Rankin, Levi Coffin, William Still, and others were known in both the white and black communities as aiders and abettors of escaped slaves. Though slave-catchers and at times law-enforcement officials watched their houses or offices, these abolitionists willingly made their views known, since escaping blacks and whites sympathetic to the abolitionist cause had to know their identities if the fugitives were to find a seat on the Liberty Line.

In the years after the Constitution was ratified, and as more slave states were admitted to the Union, the slave-holding states began to pass more restrictive laws against those still in bondage and those who were escaping. As one way to deter the forging of "pass" papers, teaching slaves to read and write was prohibited. Roadway patrols were established and authorized to apprehend escapees.

The plight of escaped slaves worsened with the passage of the Fugitive Slave Act of 1850, which placed all fugitives in free states in imminent danger. The act made it easier for the master to regain his fugitive "property." If the judge so ordered, the captured fugitive was returned to slavery in the South. U.S. marshals and deputies were charged to execute that return or face a fine of $1,000. The 1850 law also specified that "all good citizens" could be "commanded to aid and assist in the prompt and efficient execution" of the act.

As fugitives began to be seized in free states, widespread protests occurred in abolitionist circles, and more citizens began to follow their consciences, declare civil disobedience, and aid runaway slaves. They shared the views expressed by Henry David Thoreau in "Resistance to Civil Government" (1849): "heroes, patriots, martyrs, reformers in the great sense, and *men,* serve the State with their consciences also, and so necessarily resist it for the most part; and they are commonly treated by it as enemies." Indeed, many government officials regarded escaped slaves and those who aided them as criminals and enemies, especially after mobs attempted to rescue slaves awaiting return to the South.

While the exact numbers of escapees are not known, the network of Underground Railroad conductors grew over the years. According to Wilbur H. Siebert in his pioneering study *The Underground Railroad from Slavery to Freedom,* there were at least 246 conductors in Indiana and 1,539 in Ohio, the two states where Levi Coffin worked.

William Still operated in Philadelphia, where the Vigilance Committee he headed had 18 members. Pennsylvania had about 348 conductors.

A great many legends have been passed on about fugitive slaves and the conductors on the Underground Railroad, about furtive trips in wagons with the slaves hidden under produce or sacks of grain, about posses and slave-catchers on the trail of the escaped slaves, about confrontations between slave-catchers and fugitives, about the heroism of the slaves and the conductors and their allies. Many of the stories were romanticized, but two friends of slaves intimately involved with that shadowy line—Levi Coffin and William Still— wrote realistic stories about the Liberty Line to freedom. Both men were abolitionists, moved in abolitionist circles, and read abolitionist newspapers. Abolitionism deeply influenced their view of the world. They did not report pro-slavery views in order to achieve "balanced" stories. The selections in this anthology come from the writings of these two men of vision and compassion.

Levi Coffin (1798–1877), who came to be known as the president of the Underground Railroad, was born in New Garden, Guilford County, North Carolina, to Levi and Prudence Coffin, a Quaker farm family. The Coffins had come to Salisbury, Massachusetts, from England in 1642, and with other families purchased Nantucket Island in 1660. In 1773 Coffin's grandparents moved to North Carolina, a slave state. In the Quaker tradition, young Coffin's family was opposed to slavery.

Coffin was the only son in a family of seven children. He was needed on the farm and had little formal education until he was twenty-one, when he attended school briefly. He developed a clear and precise writing style, as straightforward as his orthodox Quaker religious views, lending authenticity to his accounts of his life and his efforts on behalf of blacks.

In 1824 Coffin married Catherine White, also a Quaker, and in 1826 they moved to Newport (now Fountain City), Indiana, where Coffin operated a store. Soon after their arrival in Indiana, he and his wife began to aid fugitive slaves. At least a hundred escapees a year came to the Coffins for assistance. Catherine Coffin fed and clothed those who came. She cared for them in the Coffin home, offering them emotional and physical support.

In his *Reminiscences*, Levi Coffin wrote about his wife's work with escaped slaves in Cincinnati, where the Coffins had moved in 1847:

> Our house was large and well adapted for secreting fugitives. Very often slaves would lie concealed in upper chambers for weeks without the boarders or frequent visitors at the house knowing anything about it. My wife had a quiet unconcerned way of going about her work as if nothing unusual was on hand, which was calculated to lull every suspicion of those who might be watching. . . . When my wife took food to the fugitives she generally concealed it in a basket, and put some freshly ironed garments on the top to make it look like a basketfull of clean clothes. Fugitives were not often allowed to eat in the kitchen, for fear of detection. . . .

Coffin's wife and many other abolitionist women organized sewing circles to make clothes for the fugitives, who were often in ragged garments when they first arrived at this station on the Underground Railroad. They needed shoes, which had to be bought, but the sewing circle women supplied summer and winter clothing.

Coffin became prosperous as a merchant in Newport and used his own funds and money he raised from acquaintances to meet the necessary expenses of the destitute slaves. As a major conductor on the Underground Railroad, he arranged their transportation to the next station, where a conductor would take them another part of the way to Canada or to a safe area in the North.

In his *Reminiscences*, Coffin gives few details about the escape routes he used in steering the fugitives to safety. Wilbur H. Siebert, a nineteenth-century scholar who studied the mysterious railroad, identified almost a dozen stops that slaves would have made after they left Newport for Canada. Not every one of these depots would have been used, though, for when slave hunters were in pursuit, conductors took zigzag routes to protect the passengers.

The Coffins remained active members of the Society of Friends. Levi was a proponent of Sabbath Schools for blacks; he especially wanted them to be able to read the Bible. He incorporated his religious views into his *Reminiscences*. Abolitionism was an essential part of his religious practice.

After two decades in Newport, having helped about two thousand slaves to freedom, in 1847 the Coffins moved to Cincinnati. There they aided other escaping slaves. Coffin was part of a group boycotting goods produced by slave labor, urging the use of only free-labor products. In Cincinnati he established a successful free-labor wholesale business.

Although Coffin was a pacifist, during the Civil War he did care for wounded soldiers. He also visited former slaves (called contraband) in their camps and raised money for them. After the war he was active in civil rights efforts and worked for the passage of the Fifteenth Amendment, which guaranteed that the right to vote "shall not be denied or abridged by the United States or by any State on account of race, color, or previous condition of servitude."

Coffin turned to writing his lengthy *Reminiscences* late in his life, with editorial assistance. He used his diaries and notes and his memories to reconstruct his life as an abolitionist activist. "In my own plain, simple style," he wrote, "I have endeavored to tell the stories without any exaggeration." He was aware, however, that his manuscript would contain errors, for many of the episodes he describes had taken place decades earlier. Even with the help of his diaries he could not always re-create these past events accurately. Still, his autobiography remains one of the most vivid accounts we have of the Underground Railroad.

Coffin and his wife played a role in the escape of Eliza Harris, a major character in Harriet Beecher Stowe's *Uncle Tom's Cabin*. In Stowe's fictional account, Eliza learns that her four-year-old son Harry is to be sold by Mr. Shelby to the despicable slave trader Haley, and she runs away from the Kentucky plantation to the Ohio River, taking her son with her. She is followed by Haley and the slaves Sam and Andy who constantly foil Haley's efforts to capture Eliza and Harry. Stowe's scene of Eliza's crossing the frozen river is one of the most famous escapes in American literature.

The trader caught a full glimpse of her, just as she was disappearing down the bank, and throwing himself from his horse, and calling loudly on Sam and Andy, he was after her like a hound after a deer. In that dizzy moment her feet to her scarce seemed to touch the ground, and a moment brought her to the water's edge. Right on behind her they came; and, nerved with strength such as God gives only to the desperate, with one wild cry and flying leap, she vaulted sheer over the turbid current by the shore, on to the raft of ice beyond. It was a desperate leap,—impossible to anything but madness and despair; and Haley, Sam, and Andy instinctively cried out, and lifted up their hands, as she did it.

The huge green fragment of ice on which she alighted pitched and creaked as her weight came on it, but she stayed there not a moment. With wild cries and desperate energy she leaped to another and still another cake;—stumbling,—leaping,—slipping,—springing upwards again! Her shoes were gone,—her stockings cut from her feet,—while blood marked every step; but she saw nothing, felt nothing, till dimly, as in a dream, she saw the Ohio side, and a man helping her up the bank.

Rev. John Rankin was the first conductor to help Eliza. Rankin's own account says that she had been mistreated by her Kentucky mistress and decided to flee with her small child. His story is undramatic: "The river was about to break up; the water was running upon the ice; she waded over, carrying her infant in her arms. She came to my house. The doors were not locked; she entered the kitchen, made a fire, dried her clothes, then searched for the family, found my sons and asked them to help her. They arose and took her two miles further before day." In this passage Rankin does not suggest that he told the story to Harriet Beecher.

Levi Coffin's own story of Eliza Harris and her daring escape was written long after the incident, and his memory seems to have been influenced by Stowe's novel, which he had read and admired. His account of Eliza is included in this book.

Coffin's stories are lucidly presented. His compassion is convincing. He never forgot that slavery was an historical trauma. He

Eliza and Harry on the ice floes.

worked tirelessly as a conductor, and he presents himself to the world in his *Reminiscences* as a Quaker with English heritage. However sympathetic he was to the plight of escaping slaves, he never insists that he could fully understand their world of enslavement, their way of life, or their deepest psychological motivations.

William Still (1821–1902), was born in New Jersey, youngest of the eighteen children of Levin and Charity Still. His father, born a slave in Maryland, had purchased his own freedom; Charity Still was a runaway. William Still had little formal schooling and was largely self-taught. His writing style was unadorned, but he could be eloquent in describing the injustices of slavery and the lives of those slaves who made great efforts to free themselves.

Still left home when he was twenty and worked at odd jobs until 1844, when he moved to Philadelphia. There he worked as a handyman and married. He came to be recognized in the abolitionist community as a man of great ability, and in 1847 the Philadelphia Society for the Abolition of Slavery employed him as a clerk. He then began many years of working with escaped slaves who passed through Philadelphia. He kept no notes of his early work, but after 1851 he began recording and preserving the names and circumstances of those fugitives being helped by the Society.

Still and other Society members, in their interviews with slave refugees, established the name and also the assumed name of the escapee. Skin coloration and general appearance were noted as well as overall intelligence. Still's story about Harrison Cary, arriving from Washington, D.C., shows the interview techniques Still used: Cary "was a mulatto of medium size, with a prepossessing countenance and a very smart talker." Society members asked Cary these questions:

Q. "How old are you?"
A. "Twenty-eight years of age this coming March."
Q. "To whom did you belong?"
A. "Mrs. Jane E. Ashley."
Q. "What kind of woman was she?"

A. "She was a very clever woman; never said anything out of the way."
Q. "How many servants had she?"
A. "She had no other servants."
Q. "Did you live with her?"
A. "No. I hired my time for twenty-two dollars a month."
Q. "How could you make so much money?"
A. "I was a bricklayer by trade, and ranked among the first in the city."

Cary explained that slaves out at night without passes were arrested and put in the "cage" (jail cell) and kept there until the slave's owner came to pay the fine and have the slave punished with perhaps "thirty-nine or more lashes." Cary wanted to write his own passes, and he learned to read and write in order to do so.

While Cary did not have harsh things to say about his mistress, there were distinct reasons why he had decided to leave Washington. Mrs. Ashley had a minor son, John, who according to his father's will would assume ownership of Cary upon attaining his majority. Cary thought that if John "could not take care of himself when he grew up to be a man, there was a place for all such in the poor-house." Why should Cary give his $22 a month to support a young slave owner? Cary's immediate situation had become more dangerous, for his mistress was being urged to sell him. It was time for him to get aboard the Liberty Line.

Many of the escapees interviewed by Still were married and in distress because they had been forced to leave their spouses and children behind. Because of just such hardships, Cary had resolved not to entangle himself with a family until he had obtained his freedom.

Still often included in the histories of fugitive slaves the runaway slave notices placed in Southern newspapers, legal documents, and letters from escapees. These documents and letters add authenticity to the stories he recorded. Many of the letters from escapees who reached Canada asked Still to remember them to his wife. That correspondence shows Still's wife to have been as deeply involved in aiding the former slaves as Catherine Coffin was. Coffin also forwarded to the escapees letters and parcels from their families and friends in the South who knew it was too dangerous for them to send anything to a Canadian address. He also answered queries from those attempting to locate escaped friends and relatives.

When the Fugitive Slave Act of 1850 was passed, the Pennsylvania Society for the Abolition of Slavery revived the Vigilance Committee which had been founded in 1835 "to fund aid to colored persons in distress." Still was to become chair of the committee. As Charles L. Blockson wrote in *The Underground Railroad,*

> The Vigilance Committee of Philadelphia assisted destitute fugitives by providing board and room, clothing, medicine, and money. It informed fugitives of their legal rights, gave them legal protection from kidnappers, and frequently prosecuted individuals who attempted to abduct, sell, or violate the legal rights of free blacks. Moreover, it helped runaways set up permanent homes and gave them temporary employment before their departure to Canada.

Blockson also notes that the committee carefully questioned those escapees who came seeking help: "The Underground Railroad had to be protected from spies and impostors who would expose its secret operation for fame or money."

The penalties for aiding escaped slaves were harsh, but Still kept the records of his many interviews with recently escaped slaves, hiding his notes in the attic of the Lebanon Seminary and in a graveyard. He therefore had extensive notes for the writing of his history of the Underground Railroad, which he thought of writing as early as 1867. On August 13 of that year he wrote to his daughter that he was "reading Macaulay's *History of England* with great interest," for he was intending "to write the History of the U.G.R.R. I must do a good deal of reading and thinking in order to be able to write well. I may commence my book this fall some time."

Most of the fugitives that William Still wrote about were not or did not become well known, but there were three notable exceptions: Henry Box Brown and William and Ellen Craft. Brown and William Craft wrote or participated in the writing of slave narratives that provide much information not known or used by Still. Fortunately for modern readers, these narratives are now available in carefully researched editions: *Narrative of the Life of Henry Box Brown,* with an introduction by Richard Newman and a foreword by Henry Louis Gates, Jr., and *Running a Thousand Miles for Freedom: The Escape of William and Ellen Craft from Slavery,* with a foreword and extensive biographical essay by R. J. M. Blackett.

Brown was born on a plantation about forty-five miles from Richmond, Virginia. When he was about fourteen he was taken to Richmond to work in a tobacco manufacturing plant and was there in 1831 during the excitement that followed the Nat Turner revolt. In the factory he was sometimes treated well, but one of the overseers was often especially cruel. Brown was a skilled worker and was able to set up housekeeping in a rented house once he married. He was at the mercy of his wife's owner, however, and his wife and children were sold. Agitated and distraught, he determined to be free. According to Brown's narrative, a white man named Samuel A. Smith (Brown gives him the courtesy title of Dr.) helped him escape in 1849 by fastening him into a small wooden box and shipping him to Philadelphia. According to Richard Newman, editor of the new edition of Brown's slave narrative, Brown was also helped by a free black man named James Caesar Anthony Smith.

In the box, Brown had small air holes and a bladder of water. The freight handlers often ignored the sign THIS SIDE UP, and Brown was at times upside down. After a dangerous and difficult trip, he arrived in Philadelphia, and Still was present when the lid was removed. An account of this daring escape was published in 1849, written by the white abolitionist Charles Stearns. Newman rightly notes that this slave narrative was "spoiled by Stearns' turgid style" and "scolding prose." Henry Box Brown's voice is largely missing from this lively escapade, though he was becoming a public figure and had added "Box" to his name.

In his history of the Underground Railroad, Still wrote admiringly of Brown's courage and inventiveness in escaping from Virginia, but the abolitionist's admiration of the exploit was tempered with reserve: "Indeed," Still wrote, "neither before nor after escaping did he suffer one-half what many others have experienced." Brown makes it clear how much he suffered because his wife and children were sold away from him, and it is difficult to account for Still's unsympathetic comment. Perhaps Still was upset because Henry Box Brown turned himself into something of a showman.

In 1850 Brown asked Josiah Wolcott to paint a panorama called "The Mirror of Slavery." It was what Newman refers to as "thousands of square feet of canvas" painted to show the condition of slavery. Brown then commissioned Benjamin F. Roberts to write the text and lecture for "The Condition of the Colored People in the United States." "The Mirror of Slavery" opened in the spring of 1850 and was successfully exhibited in various Northern cities, but the Fugitive Slave Act that year forced Brown to flee to England, taking with him the panorama. He was joined by his friend James Caesar Anthony Smith.

In England, Brown and Smith toured with the panorama, but their partnership lasted less than a year, ending in July 1851, though both men continued to be active on the British lecture circuit. Smith, however, began to speak against Brown, charging him with "drinking, smoking, gambling, swearing," though it would appear these charges were exaggerated. In a stunt that gained him greater public attention, Brown mailed himself from one British city to another.

Brown, though, was far more than a showman. He rewrote and performed Stephen Foster's racist song "Old Uncle Ned." Foster's version began:

Dere was an old Nigga, dey called him Uncle Ned—
He's dead long ago, long ago!
He had no wool on de top ob his head—
De place whar de wool ought to grow.
Chorus
Den lay down de shubble and de hoe,
Hang up de fiddle and de bow;
No more hard work for poor Old Ned—
He is gone whar de good Niggas go.

Brown's rewrite, with its bitter humor, was subversive:

Have you seen a man by the name of Henry Brown,
Ran away from the South to the North;
Which he would not have done but they stole all his rights,
But they'll never do the like again.

Chorus
Brown laid down the shovel and the hoe,
Down in the box he did go;
No more slave work for Henry Box Brown
In the box by express he did go.

Brown's story was not told effectively in Stearns's 1849 publication, and in 1851, in England, Brown published another version which omits much of Stearns's rhetoric. The revised text sounds and reads much more authentic. As Newman notes, "Unable to read or write and with little access to printers or publishers, Box Brown was not free from saying what other people wanted him to say. Only in England did he experience the freedom to express himself in his own way." Newman published the English edition of the narrative, never before printed in the United States.

Still tells an important part of Brown's story and includes an account of Samuel Smith's imprisonment for helping Brown escape. For a more complete and balanced report, one should turn to Newman's careful research.

Still also wrote about William and Ellen Craft, who in 1848 made a daring escape from Georgia. Ellen disguised herself as a young white man, a planter, and William accompanied her pretending to be the servant of the ill young man. After many difficulties, detailed by Still in his history of the Underground Railroad, the two arrived in Philadelphia. Still was apparently not at the abolitionist boardinghouse when the disguises were revealed, but he seems to have met the Crafts shortly thereafter. His account of their escape appears to be based on firsthand information and on later published reports. It is likely that he read their story in *Running a Thousand Miles for Freedom,* written by William and published in 1860.

Still's history of their escape lends a note of authenticity to later stories about the life of the Crafts. They made several abolitionist ap-

ELLEN CRAFT
Disguised as a young planter, she escaped to Boston in 1848,
bringing her husband with her as a valet.

pearances before settling in to a quiet life in Boston, William engaged in cabinetmaking and Ellen employed as a seamstress. Their freedom was threatened and their new life disrupted after the Fugitive Slave Act of 1850, when they foiled an attempt to capture them and return them to slavery. Still's documentation gives important information about this incident. The Crafts fled to England, and Still includes additional material about their early life there.

R. J. M. Blackett's distinguished edition of *Running a Thousand Miles for Freedom* contains a remarkably full and sympathetic account of the lives of the Crafts. For three years they were at Ockham in Surrey, an agricultural school where, Blackett writes, "students were given a basic grounding in grammar, English, writing, and music, as well as a fair sampling of Scripture studies. The students could also gain practical experience in printing, carpentry, basketmaking, and farming."

After the Crafts left Ockham, Ellen lived a quiet life in London, though she maintained her interest in abolitionist activities. William returned for a time to the lecture circuit and engaged in several not always successful business ventures. He was often away from his wife and children, once on a long and mostly unproductive stay in Dahomey.

In 1868 the Crafts left England and returned to Georgia to establish a school patterned after Ockham and to begin a farmers' cooperative for newly freed slaves. They never had enough money to implement their plans fully, even though William engaged in extensive fund-raising in Britain and in the North after their return to the United States.

In 1870 the Crafts rented Hickory Hill, a plantation in South Carolina, planted crops, and established two black schools, one for children and the other for adults. Night riders burned their house and barn. Despite great economic losses, the ever optimistic Crafts started over and leased Woodville, a plantation about twenty miles from Savannah. The school conducted there by Ellen and her son and daughter was successful. William, not trained as a rice and cotton farmer, failed all too often in his agricultural ventures. Low prices for his harvested crops and unfavorable weather during the growing season played a part in these failures. To keep the school and farm in operation, William Craft was often away in the North raising money, and eventually the Crafts purchased Woodville. They also had to deal with unfriendly white neighbors in Georgia.

Still, though devoted to his humanitarian work for the Underground Railroad, was also a family man who did not neglect his wife and children. He seems to have been offended by William Craft's sustained absences from his wife and children in Georgia. In 1873 Still wrote his brother that two of the Crafts' sons had arrived penniless at his home. They had been in Washington and were on their way to Boston to meet their father. Still asked his brother to make inquiries about the "mysterious man" who left his family in Georgia and spent most of his time in Boston. Blackett rightly observes that William Craft "never tried to calm his friends' concerns; to him, the cause took precedence over family responsibilities."

The Crafts were always pressed for money, often having to mortgage their property. Their school eventually had to be closed, their children began to leave the plantation, and Ellen, always a stabilizing force, died in 1891. The experiment at Woodville struggled on for a few more years before it was taken over by creditors in 1900, the same year that William died.

Blackett makes a strong and convincing case for the importance of William and Ellen Craft's achievements: "Through their daring escape from Macon and their activities in Boston and then in England, the Crafts contributed immeasurably to Anglo-American abolitionism. Their escape dramatized the moral turpitude of American slavery, and their attempted recapture heightened sectional conflict in the years before the Civil War." Blackett writes that they "displayed an indomitable spirit, always willing to take risks in order to achieve their objectives." They returned to the unfriendly environment of Georgia because they were determined "to employ their knowledge and skills for the elevation of the freedman." Blackett, with a perspective based on more information than Still had, could reasonably be generous in his assessment of the Crafts.

In his accounts of escapees, Still seems to be most sympathetic to courageous and resourceful men and women fugitives who lived quiet, productive lives in freedom. A free black man, Still followed that path himself.

Like Levi Coffin, Still was an astute businessman. He bought real estate, established a store that sold stoves and coal, and owned a coal yard. He successfully published his massive *The Underground Rail Road*, selling it by subscription through agents. The 1872 edition was followed by additional printings in 1879 and 1883.

During and after the Civil War, Still worked to end racial discrimination and promote the civil rights of African Americans. He was public spirited and involved in the management of homes for the aged and an orphanage for the children of black sailors and soldiers.

Like Coffin, Still supported the temperance movement. And, like Coffin, he was a religious man—a Presbyterian, like the abolitionists John Rankin and John Cross. Coffin, Still, Rankin, and Cross were all interested in education: Coffin and Still were particularly concerned with establishing Sabbath Schools to teach blacks to read and write.

"Still's book, *The Underground Rail Road,*" wrote Larry Gara in the Still entry in *American National Biography,* "was unique. The only work on that subject written by an African American, it was also the only day-by-day record of the working of a vigilance committee." In the Preface to his book, Still wrote that he made efforts "to resort to no coloring to make the book seem romantic" and to concentrate on the lives and stories of those "making their way from Slavery to Freedom, with the horrors of the Fugitive Slave-law staring them in the face." In his actions and writings Still shows that he understood the psychology and the aspirations of fugitive slaves.

Charles L. Blockson, in *The Underground Railroad,* insists, "A serious distortion has been an over-emphasis on the amount of assistance rendered by white abolitionists, who wrote a great deal on the subject. This tended to make the people whom the railroad was designed to aid—the fugitive slaves—seem either invisible or passive and helpless without aid from others." Although this statement contains elements of truth, Levi Coffin, John Rankin, and many other white abolitionists did not regard most runaways as "passive and helpless." That there were strong racist attitudes pervading American society during slavery days cannot be denied, and without doubt some abolitionists shared some of those views, even though they may have attempted to overcome them.

Levi Coffin cast his account of the Underground Railroad as reminiscences and therefore had much to report on his life as a conductor. This simply dressed, plainspoken man describes his initial interest as a young child in helping blacks and is never reluctant to describe the Quaker influences on his life and his abolitionist efforts. He relished outwitting slave owners and their posses searching for runaways, but he was a man of peace, never armed, unafraid of Southern ruffians who threatened to harm him.

William Still was a child of parents born into slavery, and he knew from them the horrors of that institution. He emphasizes in his book the struggles of blacks to gain freedom, and he underplays his own activities on their behalf. In his long book he writes little about himself, and we know of his Underground Railroad efforts, and of those of his wife, most often from the letters those grateful runaways wrote to Still after they reached safety. Unlike Coffin, Still does not write about his religious views and the part they played in his abolitionist efforts. Still treats the religious views of slave owners with derision, and he often uses satire and irony when writing about them, something Coffin, a Quaker, usually refrains from doing. Still also writes about the slaves who were armed and ready and willing to fight for their freedom against armed white posses and slave-catchers. Coffin generally omits such episodes of violence.

From Levi Coffin's *Reminiscences* and William Still's *The Underground Rail Road* we have chosen representative stories about conductors on the Liberty Line and about those passengers who rode it. Together these two accounts, with their different viewpoints, give a large-scale picture of the shadowy railroad and courageous conductors and blacks who sought freedom. In these stories the conductors and escaping slaves speak directly to us. Their accounts are part of our national heritage and deserve to be read, reread, and remembered.

Reminiscences

of

Levi Coffin

THE REPUTED PRESIDENT OF THE
UNDERGROUND RAILROAD

I.

Conversion to Abolitionism—Stephen, the Kidnapped Negro—The Captured Slave—Fugitives in Concealment— The White Slave

⫸ I date my conversion to Abolitionism from an incident which occurred when I was about seven years old. It made a deep and lasting impression on my mind, and created that horror of the cruelties of slavery which has been the motive of so many actions of my life. At the time of which I speak, Virginia and Maryland were the principal slave-rearing States, and to a great extent supplied the Southern market. Free negroes in Pennsylvania were frequently kidnapped or decoyed into these States, then hurried away to Georgia, Alabama, or Louisiana, and sold. The gangs were handcuffed and chained together, and driven by a man on horseback, who flourished a long whip, such as is used in driving cattle, and goaded the reluctant and weary when their feet lagged on the long journey. One day I was by the roadside where my father was chopping wood, when I saw such a gang approaching along the new Salisbury road. The coffle of slaves came first, chained in couples on each side of a long chain which extended between them; the driver was some distance behind, with the wagon of supplies. My father addressed the slaves pleasantly, and then asked: "Well, boys, why do they chain you?" One of the men, whose countenance betrayed unusual intelligence and whose expression denoted the deepest sadness, replied: "They have taken us away

Levi Coffin

from our wives and children, and they chain us lest we should make our escape and go back to them." My childish sympathy and interest were aroused, and when the dejected procession had passed on, I turned to my father and asked many questions concerning them, why they were taken away from their families, etc. In simple words, suited to my comprehension, my father explained to me the meaning of slavery, and, as I listened, the thought arose in my mind—"How terribly we should feel if father were taken away from us."

This was the first awakening of that sympathy with the oppressed, which, together with a strong hatred of oppression and injustice in every form, were the motives that influenced my whole after-life. Another incident of my boyhood is indelibly engraved on my mind. I accompanied my father one spring to the famous shad fishery at the narrows of the Yadkin River, a spot of wild and romantic scenery,

Catherine Coffin

where the stream breaks through a spur of the mountains and goes foaming and dashing down its rocky bed in a succession of rapids. Every spring, when the shad ascended the river, many people resorted to the place to obtain fish. They brought with them a variety of merchandise, saddlery, crockery-ware, etc., and remained in camp some time, buying and selling. The fishery was owned by two brothers named Crump. They were slaveholders, and sometimes allowed their slaves the privilege of fishing after night and disposing of the fish thus obtained, on their own account. A slave, who had availed himself of this privilege, disposed of the fish he caught to my father. Next morning he came to the place where we were preparing breakfast, and entered into conversation with my father, speaking of the fish he had sold him, and asking if he would take more on the same terms. Noticing this, and thinking it a piece of presuming familiarity and impertinence, on the part of the negro, a young man, nephew of the Crumps, seized a fagot from the fire and struck the negro a furious blow across the head, baring the skull, covering his back and breast with blood, and his head with fire; swearing at the same time that he would allow no such impudence from niggers. My father protested against the act, and I was so deeply moved that I left my breakfast untasted, and going off by myself gave vent to my feelings in sobs and tears.

A few such instances of "man's inhumanity to man" intensified my hatred of slavery, and inspired me to devote myself to the cause of the helpless and oppressed, and enter upon that line of humane effort, which I pursued for more than fifty years. I would still be engaged in it had not Abraham Lincoln broken up the business by proclamation in 1863.

STEPHEN, THE KIDNAPPED NEGRO

The first opportunity for aiding a slave occurred when I was about fifteen years old. It was a custom in North Carolina, at that time, to make a "frolic" of any special work, like corn husking, log-rolling, etc. The neighbors would assemble at the place appointed, and with willing hearts and busy hands soon complete the work. Then followed the supper and the merry-making, and the night was in

"The wee sma' hours ayant the twal,"

before the lights were out and the company gone.

At a gathering of this kind, a corn husking at Dr. Caldwell's, I was present. The neighbors assembled about dark, bringing their slaves with them. The negroes were assigned a place at one end of the heap, the white people took their place at the other, and all went to work, enlivening their labor with songs and merry talk.

A slave-dealer, named Stephen Holland, had arrived in the neighborhood a short time before, with a coffle of slaves, on his way to the South, and as this was his place of residence, he stopped for a few days before proceeding on his journey. He brought with him his band of slaves to help his neighbor husk corn, and I was much interested in them. When the white people went in to supper I remained behind to talk with the strange negroes, and see if I could render them any service. In conversation I learned that one of the negroes, named Stephen, was free born, but had been kidnapped and sold into slavery. Till he became of age he had been indentured to Edward Lloyd, a Friend, living near Philadelphia. When his apprenticeship was ended, he had been hired by a man to help drive a flock of sheep to Baltimore. After reaching that place he had been seized one night as he was asleep in the negro house of a tavern, gagged and bound, then placed in a close carriage, and driven rapidly across the line into Virginia, where he was confined the next night in a cellar. He had then been sold for a small sum to Holland, who was taking him to the Southern market, where he expected to realize a large sum from his sale. I became deeply interested in his story, and began to think how I could help him to regain his freedom. Remembering Dr. Caldwell's Tom, a trusty negro, whom I knew well, I imparted to him my wishes, and desired him, if it could be arranged, to bring Stephen to my father's the next night. They came about midnight, and my father wrote down the particulars of Stephen's case, and took the address of the Lloyds. The next day he wrote to them, giving an account of Stephen and his whereabouts. In two weeks from that time, Hugh Lloyd, a brother of Edward Lloyd, arrived by stage in Greensboro. Procuring conveyance, he came to my father's, and there learned that Stephen had been taken southward by the slave-dealer Holland. Next day being regular meeting-day at the Friends Meeting-House, at New Garden, the case was laid before the men after meeting, and two of them, Dr. George Swain and Henry Macy, volunteered to accompany Hugh Lloyd in search of Stephen.

A sum of money was made up for the expense of their journey, and Lloyd was furnished with horse and saddle and the necessary equipments. The party found Stephen in Georgia, where he had been sold by Holland, who had gone farther South. A suit was instituted to gain possession of him, but the laws of that State required proof, in such instances, that the mother had been free, and Hugh Lloyd was too young to give this proof. So the matter was referred to the next term of court, security being given by Stephen's master that he should be produced when wanted. Lloyd returned North, and sent affidavits and free papers giving proof in the case, and in six months Stephen was liberated and returned home. The man who had hired him to drive the sheep to Baltimore had, in the meantime, been arrested on the charge of kidnapping, but as Stephen was the only prosecuting witness, the suit could not go on while he was absent. The man's friends took him out of jail on a writ of *habeas corpus* and gave bond for his appearance at court, but he preferred forfeiting his bond to standing the trial, and fled the country before Stephen returned.

THE CAPTURED SLAVE

But I was not always so fortunate as to be able to render assistance to the objects of my sympathy. Sometimes I witnessed scenes of cruelty and injustice and had to stand passively by. The following is an instance of that kind: I had been sent one day on an errand to a place in the neighborhood, called Clemen's Store, and was returning home along the Salem road, when I met a party of movers, with wagons, teams, slaves and household goods, on their way to another State. After passing them I came to a blacksmith's shop, in front of which were several men, talking and smoking, in idle chat, and proceeding on my way I met a negro man trudging along slowly on foot, carrying a bundle. He inquired of me regarding the party of movers; asked how far they were ahead, etc. I told him "About half a mile," and as he passed on, the thought occurred to me that this man was probably a runaway slave who was following the party of movers. I had heard of instances when families were separated—the wife and children being taken by their owners to another part of the country—of the husband and father following the party of emigrants, keeping a short distance behind the train of wagons during the day, and creeping up to the camp at night, close enough for his wife to see him and bring him food. A few days afterward I learned that this man had been stopped and questioned by the party of men at the blacksmith's shop, that he had produced a pass, but they being satisfied that it was a forgery had lodged him in jail at Greensboro, and sent word to his master concerning him. A week or two afterward I was sent to a blacksmith's shop, at Greensboro, to get some work done. The slave's master had, that very day, arrived and taken possession of him, and brought him to the blacksmith's shop to get some irons put on him before starting back to his home. While a chain was being riveted around the negro's neck, and handcuffs fastened on his wrists, his master upbraided him for having run away. He asked:

"Wer'n't you well treated?"

"Yes, massa."

"Then what made you run away?"

"My wife and children were taken away from me, massa, and I think as much of them as you do of yours, or any white man does of his. Their massa tried to buy me too, but you would not sell me, so when I saw them go away, I followed." The mere recital of his words can convey little idea of the pitiful and pathetic manner in which they were uttered; his whole frame trembled, and the glance of piteous, despairing appeal he turned upon his master would have melted any heart less hard than stone.

The master said, "I've always treated you well, trusting you with my keys, and treating you more like a confidential servant than a slave, but *now* you shall know what slavery is. Just wait till I get you back home!" He then tried to make the negro tell where he had got his pass, who wrote it for him, etc., but he refused to betray the person who had befriended him. The master threatened him with the severest punishment, but he persisted in his refusal. Then torture was tried, in order to force the name from him. Laying the slave's fettered hand on the blacksmith's anvil, the master struck it with a hammer until the blood settled under the finger nails. The negro winced under each cruel blow, but said not a word. As I stood by and watched this scene, my heart swelled with indignation, and I longed to rescue the slave and punish the master. I was not converted to peace principles then, and I felt like fighting for the slave. One end of the chain, riveted to the negro's neck, was made fast to the axle of his master's buggy, then the master sprang in and drove off at a sweeping trot, compelling the slave to run at full speed or fall and be dragged by his neck. I watched them till they disappeared in the distance, and as long as I could see them, the slave was running.

FUGITIVES IN CONCEALMENT

Runaway slaves used frequently to conceal themselves in the woods and thickets in the vicinity of New Garden, waiting opportunities to make their escape to the North, and I generally learned their places of concealment and rendered them all the service in my power. My father, in common with other farmers in that part of the country, allowed his hogs to run in the woods, and I often went out to feed them. My sack of corn generally contained supplies of bacon and corn bread for the slaves, and many a time I sat in the thickets with them as they hungrily devoured my bounty, and listened to the stories they told of hard masters and cruel treatment, or spoke in language, simple and rude, yet glowing with native eloquence, of the glorious hope of freedom which animated their spirits in the darkest hours, and sustained them under the sting of the lash.

These outlying slaves knew where I lived, and, when reduced to extremity of want or danger, often came to my room, in the silence and darkness of night, to obtain food or assistance. In my efforts to aid these fugitives I had a zealous co-worker in my friend and cousin, Vestal Coffin, who was then, and continued to the time of his death—a few years later—a stanch friend to the slave.

Vestal was several years older than I, was married and had the care of a family, but, in the busiest season of work, could find time to co-operate with me in all my endeavors to aid runaway slaves. We often met at night in a thicket where a fugitive was concealed, to counsel in regard to his prospects and lay plans for getting him safely started to the North. We employed General Hamilton's Sol, a gray-haired, trusty old negro, to examine every coffle of slaves to which he could gain access, and ascertain if there were any kidnapped negroes among them. When such a case was discovered, Sol would manage to bring the person, by night, to some rendezvous appointed, in the pine thickets or the depths of the woods, and there Vestal and I would meet them and have an interview. There was always a risk in holding such meetings, for the law in the South inflicted heavy penalties on any one who should aid or abet a fugitive slave in escaping, and the patrollers, or mounted officers, frequently passed along the road near our place of concealment. When information had been obtained from kidnapped negroes regarding the circumstances of their capture, Vestal Coffin wrote to their friends, and in many cases succeeded in getting them liberated. In this way a negro man of family and means, who had been abducted from Pennsylvania and taken to New Orleans and sold, was finally restored to his friends. Obtaining through Vestal Coffin a knowledge of his whereabouts, they brought suit against his owners and gained his liberty. . . .

THE WHITE SLAVE

In the following story I was no way concerned, but the incidents came under my observation, and I can well remember the feelings of deepest sympathy and indignation which it aroused in our neighborhood at the time of its occurrence. It shows one of the cruelest phases of slavery, and gives one of the many instances in which the deepest suffering was inflicted on those who merited it by no act of their own, but received the curse by inheritance.

A slaveholder, living in Virginia, owned a beautiful slave woman, who was almost white. She became the mother of a child, a little boy, in whose veins ran the blood of her master, and the closest observer could not detect in its appearance any trace of African descent. He grew to be two or three years of age, a most beautiful child and the idol of his mother's heart, when the master concluded, for family reasons, to send him away. He placed him in the care of a friend living in Guilford County, North Carolina, and made an agreement that he should receive a common-school education, and at a suitable age be taught some useful trade. Years passed; the child grew to manhood, and having received a good common-school education, and learned the shoemaker's trade, he married an estimable young white woman, and had a family of five or six children. He had not the slightest knowledge of the taint of African blood in his veins, and no one in the neighborhood knew that he was the son of an octoroon slave woman. He made a comfortable living for his family, was a good citizen, a member of the Methodist Church, and was much respected by all who knew him. In course of time his father, the Virginian slaveholder, died, and when the executors came to settle up the estate, they remembered the little white boy, the son of the slave woman, and knowing that by law—such law!—he belonged to the estate, and must be by this time a valuable piece of property, they resolved to gain possession of him. After much inquiry and search they learned of his whereabouts, and the heir of the estate, accompanied by an administrator, went to Guilford County, North Carolina, to claim his half-brother as a slave. Without making themselves known to him, they sold him to a negro trader, and gave a bill of sale, preferring to have a sum in ready money, instead of a servant who might prove very valuable, but who would, without doubt, give them a great deal of trouble. He had been free all his life, and they knew he would not readily yield to the yoke of bondage. All this time the victim was entirely unconscious of the cruel fate in store for him.

His wife had been prostrated by a fever then prevalent in the neighborhood, and he had waited upon her and watched by her bedside, until he was worn out with exhaustion and loss of sleep. Several neighbor women coming in one evening to watch with the invalid, he surrendered her to their care, and retired to seek the rest he so much needed. That night the slave-dealer came with a gang of ruffians, burst into the house and seized their victim as he lay asleep, bound him, after heroic struggles on his part, and dragged him away. When he demanded the cause of his seizure, they showed him the bill of sale they had received, and informed him that he was a slave. In this rude, heartless manner the intelligence that he belonged to the African race was first imparted to him, and the crushing weight of his cruel destiny came upon him when totally unprepared. His captors hurried him out of the neighborhood, and took him toward the Southern slave markets. To get him black enough to sell without question, they washed his face in tan ooze, and kept him tied in the sun, and to complete his resemblance to a mulatto, they cut his hair short and seared it with a hot iron to make it curly. He was sold in Georgia or Alabama, to a hard master, by whom he was cruelly treated.

Several months afterward he succeeded in escaping, and made his way back to Guilford County, North Carolina. Here he learned that his wife had died a few days after his capture, the shock of that calamity having hastened her death, and that his children were scattered among the neighbors. His master, thinking that he would return to his old home, came in pursuit of him with hounds, and chased him through the thickets and swamps. He evaded the dogs by wading in a mill-pond, and climbing a tree, where he remained all night. Next day he made his way to the house of Stanton White (afterward my father-in-law), where he remained several days. Dr. George Swain, a man of much influence in the community, had an interview with him, and, hearing the particulars of his seizure, said he thought the proceedings were illegal. He held a consultation with several lawyers, and instituted proceedings in his behalf. But the unfortunate victim of man's cruelty did not live to regain his freedom. He had been exposed and worried so much, trailed by dogs and forced to lie in swamps and thickets, that his health was broken down and he died before the next term of court. . . .

II.

Marriage—Removal to Indiana—I
Locate at Newport and Engage in
Mercantile Business—Underground
Railroad Work—Difficulties and
Dangers of the Work—Trip to North
Carolina—Heart-rending Scene
at a Slave Auction

⊂⊋ On the 28th day of tenth month, 1824, I was married to
Catherine White, daughter of Stanton and Sarah White. We were
brought up in the same neighborhood, and had been acquainted from
childhood. She belonged to the Religious Society of Friends, and was
then a member of Hopewell Monthly Meeting, to which place her father had removed a few years before, from his former residence near
New Garden. We were married at Hopewell Meeting-House, after
the manner and custom of Friends.

My wedding-day was my twenty-sixth birthday; my wife was
twenty-one the preceding month. Our attachment to each other was
of long standing. She was an amiable and attractive young woman of
lively, buoyant spirits. Her heart has ever been quick to respond to the
cry of distress, and she has been an able and efficient helper to me in
all my efforts on behalf of the fugitive slaves, and a cheerful sharer in
all the toils, privations and dangers which we have, in consequence,
been called upon to endure.

Soon after marriage I rented a house near my school, and here we first went to housekeeping. My school closed early in the spring, and I concluded to rest awhile from the arduous duties of teaching.

Thinking that my health would be improved by the open-air exercise of farming, and having a very favorable offer made me of a comfortable house, without charge, in that neighborhood, and as much ground as I wished to cultivate, I prepared to engage in farming. This prospect was pleasant to us both, as my wife and I had been brought up on farms. The house was tendered us by our friend and neighbor Shields Moore, who now lives in Indiana. We went to work in good spirits and soon had a garden planted and a crop in. But my plan for farming soon came to an end.

A new school-house had just been completed, about two miles north of Deep River Meeting-House, in a thickly settled neighborhood of Friends. This settlement was called Nazareth, and the school-house received the same name. There was a large number of young people in the neighborhood, for whose benefit the parents were anxious to establish a good school. A committee, consisting of Abel Coffin, Thaddeus Gardner, Zacharias Coffin and Peter Hunt, visited me and asked me to take the school. . . .

This was the largest and most interesting school that I ever taught. During this year I was also engaged in Sabbath-school work. . . .

When my school closed, . . . I was then preparing to move to the State of Indiana. . . .

In the early part of the ninth month, 1826, we took a final leave of North Carolina. My parents had emigrated to Indiana the previous year, and I was the last one of our family to go. My family at this time consisted of myself, my wife, and our son Jesse, about a year old. My wife's parents were not then prepared to move, but followed the next year. On our way to Indiana we had the company of my wife's cousin, Elias Jessup, and his little family.

We made the journey in light wagons, with good teams, and had a pleasant trip. We took the shortest route, called the Kanawha road, and arrived at our destination in four weeks from the time of starting. We located at Newport, Wayne County, Indiana, where we lived for more than twenty years. This village was in the midst of a large settlement of Friends, and a Quarterly Meeting was then established at New Garden Meeting-House, about a half mile from the village. I bought property in Newport, and finding that there was a good opening there for a mercantile business, I concluded to engage in it. I went to Cincinnati and purchased a small stock of goods and opened a store. This venture was successful, and I increased my stock and varied my assortment of goods until a large retail business was established.

The next year I commenced cutting pork in a small way, besides carrying on my other business. This I continued to do, enlarging my operations every year, and kept it up as long as I remained in Newport.

In the year 1836, I built an oil mill and manufactured linseed oil. Notwithstanding all this multiplicity of business, I was never too busy to engage in Underground Railroad affairs. Soon after we located at Newport, I found that we were on a line of the U. G. R. R. Fugitives often passed through that place, and generally stopped among the colored people. There was in that neighborhood a number of families of free colored people, mostly from North Carolina, who were the descendants of slaves who had been liberated by Friends many years before, and sent to free States at the expense of North Carolina Yearly Meeting. I learned that the fugitive slaves who took refuge with these people were often pursued and captured, the colored people not being very skillful in concealing them, or shrewd in making arrangements to forward them to Canada. I was pained to hear of the capture of these fugitives, and inquired of some of the Friends in our village why they did not take them in and secrete them, when they were pursued, and then aid them on their way to Canada? I found that they were afraid of the penalty of the law. I told them that I read in the Bible when I was a boy that it was right to take in the stranger and administer to those in distress, and that I thought it was always safe to do right. The Bible, in bidding us to feed the hungry and clothe the naked, said nothing about color, and I should try to follow out the teachings of that good book. I was willing to receive and aid as many fugitives as were disposed to come to my house. I knew that my wife's feelings and sympathies regarding this matter were the same as mine, and that she was willing to do her part. It soon became known to the colored people in our neighborhood and others, that our house was a depot where the hunted and harassed fugitive journeying northward, on the Underground Railroad, could find succor and sympathy. It also became known at other depots on the various lines that converged at Newport.

In the winter of 1826–27, fugitives began to come to our house, and as it became more widely known on different routes that the slaves fleeing from bondage would find a welcome and shelter at our house, and be forwarded safely on their journey, the number increased. Friends in the neighborhood, who had formerly stood aloof from the work, fearful of the penalty of the law, were encouraged to engage in it when they saw the fearless manner in which I acted, and the success that attended my efforts. They would contribute to clothe the fugitives, and would aid in forwarding them on their way, but were timid about sheltering them under their roof; so that part of the work devolved on us. Some seemed really glad to see the work go on, if somebody else would do it. Others doubted the propriety of it, and tried to discourage me, and dissuade me from running such risks. They manifested great concern for my safety and pecuniary interests, telling me that such a course of action would injure my business and perhaps ruin me; that I ought to consider the welfare of my family; and warning me that my life was in danger, as there were many threats made against me by the slave-hunters and those who sympathized with them.

After listening quietly to these counselors, I told them that I felt no condemnation for anything that I had ever done for the fugitive slaves. If by doing my duty and endeavoring to fulfill the injunctions of the Bible, I injured my business, then let my business go. As to my safety, my life was in the hands of my Divine Master, and I felt that I had his approval. I had no fear of the danger that seemed to threaten my life or my business. If I was faithful to duty, and honest and industrious, I felt that I would be preserved, and that I could make enough to support my family. At one time there came to see me a good old Friend, who was apparently very deeply concerned for my welfare. He said he was as much opposed to slavery as I was, but thought it very wrong to harbor fugitive slaves. No one there knew of what crimes they were guilty; they might have killed their masters, or committed some other atrocious deed, then those who sheltered them, and aided them in their escape from justice would indirectly be accomplices. He mentioned other objections which he wished me to consider, and then talked for some time, trying to convince me of the errors of my ways. I heard him patiently until he had relieved his mind of the burden upon it, and then asked if he thought the Good Samaritan stopped to inquire whether the man who fell among thieves was guilty of any crime before he attempted to help him? I asked him if he were to see a stranger who had fallen into the ditch would he not help him out until satisfied that he had committed no atrocious deed? These, and many other questions which I put to him, he did not seem able to answer satisfactorily. He was so perplexed and confused that I really pitied the good old man, and advised him to go home and read his Bible thoroughly, and pray over it, and I thought his concern about my aiding fugitive slaves would be removed from his mind, and that he would feel like helping me in the work. We parted in good feeling, and he always manifested warm friendship toward me until the end of his days.

Many of my pro-slavery customers left me for a time, my sales were diminished, and for a while my business prospects were discouraging, yet my faith was not shaken, nor my efforts for the slaves lessened. New customers soon came in to fill the places of those who had left me. New settlements were rapidly forming to the north of us, and our own was filling up with emigrants from North Carolina, and other States. My trade increased, and I enlarged my business. I was blessed in all my efforts and succeeded beyond my expectations. The Underground Railroad business increased as time advanced, and it was attended with heavy expenses, which I could not have borne had not my affairs been prosperous. I found it necessary to keep a team and a wagon always at command, to convey the fugitive slaves on their journey. Sometimes, when we had large companies, one or two other teams and wagons were required. These journeys had to be made at night, often through deep mud and bad roads, and along by-ways that were seldom traveled. Every precaution to evade pursuit had to be used, as the hunters were often on the track, and sometimes ahead of the slaves. We had different routes for sending the fugitives to depots, ten, fifteen, or twenty miles distant, and when we heard of slave-hunters having passed on one road, we forwarded our passengers by another.

In some instances where we learned that the pursuers were ahead of them, we sent a messenger and had the fugitives brought back to my house to remain in concealment until the bloodhounds in human shape had lost the trail and given up the pursuit.

I soon became extensively known to the friends of the slaves, at different points on the Ohio River, where fugitives generally crossed, and to those northward of us on the various routes leading to Canada. Depots were established on the different lines of the Underground Railroad, south and north of Newport, and a perfect understanding was maintained between those who kept them. Three principal lines from the South converged at my house; one from Cincinnati, one from Madison, and one from Jeffersonville, Indiana. The roads were always in running order, the connections were good, the conductors active and zealous, and there was no lack of passengers. Seldom a week passed without our receiving passengers by this mysterious road. We found it necessary to be always prepared to receive such company and properly care for them. We knew not what night or what hour of the night we would be roused from slumber by a gentle rap at the door. That was the signal announcing the arrival of a train of the Underground Railroad, for the locomotive did not whistle, nor make any unnecessary noise. I have often been awakened by this sig-nal, and sprang out of bed in the dark and opened the door. Outside in the cold or rain, there would be a two-horse wagon loaded with fugitives, perhaps the greater part of them women and children. I would invite them, in a low tone, to come in, and they would follow me into the darkened house without a word, for we knew not who might be watching and listening. When they were all safely inside and the door fastened, I would cover the windows, strike a light and build a good fire. By this time my wife would be up and preparing victuals for them, and in a short time the cold and hungry fugitives would be made comfortable. I would accompany the conductor of the train to the stable, and care for the horses, that had, perhaps, been driven twenty-five or thirty miles that night, through the cold and rain. The fugitives would rest on pallets before the fire the rest of the night. Frequently, wagon-loads of passengers from the different lines have met at our house, having no previous knowledge of each other. The companies varied in number, from two or three fugitives to seventeen.

The care of so many necessitated much work and anxiety on our part, but we assumed the burden of our own will and bore it cheerfully. It was never too cold or stormy, or the hour of night too late for my wife to rise from sleep, and provide food and comfortable lodging for the fugitives. Her sympathy for those in distress never tired, and her efforts in their behalf never abated. This work was kept up during the time we lived at Newport, a period of more than twenty years. The number of fugitives varied considerably in different years, but the annual average was more than one hundred. They generally came to us destitute of clothing, and were often barefooted. Clothing must be collected and kept on hand, if possible, and money must be raised to buy shoes, and purchase goods to make garments for women and children. The young ladies in the neighborhood organized a sewing society, and met at our house frequently, to make clothes for the fugitives.

Sometimes when the fugitives came to us destitute, we kept them several days, until they could be provided with comfortable clothes. This depended on the circumstances of danger. If they had come a long distance and had been out several weeks or months—as was sometimes the case—and it was not probable that hunters were on their track, we thought it safe for them to remain with us until fitted for traveling through the thinly settled country to the North. Sometimes fugitives have come to our house in rags, foot-sore and toil-worn, and almost wild, having been out for several months traveling at night, hiding in canebrakes or thickets during the day, often being lost and making little headway at night, particularly in cloudy weather, when the north star could not be seen, sometimes almost perishing for want of food, and afraid of every white person they saw, even after they came into a free State, knowing that slaves were often captured and taken back after crossing the Ohio River.

Such as these we have kept until they were recruited in strength, provided with clothes, and able to travel. When they first came to us they were generally unwilling to tell their stories, or let us know what part of the South they came from. They would not give their names, or the names of their masters, correctly, fearing that they would be betrayed. In several instances fugitives came to our house sick from exhaustion and exposure, and lay several weeks. One case was that of a woman and her two children—little girls. Hearing that her children were to be sold away from her, she determined to take them with her and attempt to reach Canada. She had heard that Canada was a place where all were free, and that by traveling toward the north star she could reach it. She managed to get over the Ohio River with her two little girls, and then commenced her long and toilsome journey northward. Fearing to travel on the road, even at night, lest she should meet somebody, she made her way through the woods and across fields, living on fruits and green corn, when she could procure them, and sometimes suffering severely for lack of food. Thus she wandered on, and at last reached our neighborhood. Seeing a cabin where some colored people lived she made her way to it. The people received her kindly, and at once conducted her to our house. She was so exhausted by the hardships of her long journey, and so weakened by hunger, having denied herself to feed her children, that she soon became quite sick. Her children were very tired, but soon recovered their strength, and were in good health. They had no shoes nor clothing except what they had on, and that was in tatters. Dr. Henry H. Way was called in, and faithfully attended the sick woman, until her health was restored. Then the little party were provided with good clothing and other comforts, and were sent on their way to Canada.

Dr. Way was a warm friend to the fugitive slaves, and a hearty coworker with me in anti-slavery matters. The number of those who were friendly to the fugitives increased in our neighborhood as time passed on. Many were willing to aid in clothing them and helping them on their way, and a few were willing to aid in secreting them, but the depot seemed to be established at my house.

Notwithstanding the many threats of slave-hunters and the strong prejudices of pro-slavery men, I continued to prosper and gained a business influence in the community. Some of my customers, who had left me several years before on account of my anti-slavery sentiments, began to deal with me again. I had been elected a director in the Richmond branch of the State Bank, and was re-elected annually for six or seven years, by the stockholders, to represent our district. When any one wished accommodation from the bank, much depended on the director from the district where the applicant lived. His word or influence would generally decide the matter. The remembrance of this seemed to hold a check on some of the pro-slavery men of our neighborhood. They wished to retain my friendship, and did not openly oppose my U. G. R. R. work as they might otherwise have done. My business influence no doubt operated in some degree to shield me from the attacks of the slave-hunters. These men often threatened to kill me, and at various times offered a reward for my head. I often received anonymous letters warning me that my store, pork-house, and dwelling would be burned to the ground, and one letter, mailed in Kentucky, informed me that a body of armed men were then on their way to Newport to destroy the town. The letter named the night in which the work would be accomplished, and warned me to flee from the place, for if I should be taken my life would pay for my crimes against Southern slaveholders. I had become so accustomed to threats and warnings, that this made no impression on me—struck no terror to my heart. The most of the inhabitants of our village were Friends, and their principles were those of peace and non-resistance. They were not alarmed at the threat to destroy the town, and on the night appointed retired to their beds as usual and slept peacefully. We placed no sentinels to give warning of danger, and had no extra company at our house to guard our lives. We retired to rest at the usual hour, and were not disturbed during the night. In the morning the buildings were all there—there was no smell of fire, no sign of the terrible destruction threatened. I heard of only one person who was alarmed, and he did not live in town.

The fright of this man created considerable amusement at the time and was not soon forgotten. He was a poor laborer, who lived a mile and a half from Newport, in a cabin which he had built in the woods. About half a mile east of his place, two roads crossed each other, one of them leading to Newport, and near the cross-roads was a large pond of water. This incident occurred in the spring of the year. Having heard that on a certain night the town of Newport was to be destroyed by an army from Kentucky, this man was listening, at the time appointed, for the sound of the approaching army. Soon after dark he was sure he heard martial music near the cross-roads. He hastened to town with all speed, and came into my store, almost out of breath, to give the alarm. We laughed at him, and told him that he heard the noise of frogs in that pond of water, but he would not be convinced. To satisfy him, a young man present said he would mount his horse and go with him to hear the music. He went, and soon returned and informed us that the frogs were making a lively noise in the pond in honor of the return of spring; that was all the music to be heard. The laborer was so chagrined at his ludicrous mistake, that he did not show himself in town for some time.

Slave-hunters often passed through our town and sometimes had hired ruffians with them from Richmond, and other neighboring places. They knew me well, and knew that I harbored slaves and aided them to escape, but they never ventured to search my premises, or molest me in any way.

I had many employees about my place of business, and much company about my house, and it seemed too public a place for fugitives to hide. These slave-hunters knew that if they committed any trespass, or went beyond the letter of the law, I would have them arrested, and they knew also that I had many friends who would stand at my back and aid me in prosecuting them. Thus, my business influence and large acquaintance afforded me protection in my labors for the oppressed fugitives. I expressed my anti-slavery sentiments with boldness on every occasion. I told the sympathizers with slave-hunters that I intended to shelter as many runaway slaves as came to my house, and aid them on their way; and advised them to be careful how they interfered with my work. They might get themselves into difficulty if they undertook to capture slaves from my premises, and become involved in a legal prosecution, for most of the arrests of slaves were unlawful. The law required that a writ should be obtained, and a proof that the slave was their property before they could take him away, and if they proceeded contrary to these requirements, and attempted to enter my house, I would have them arrested as kidnappers. These expressions, uttered frequently, had, I thought, a tendency to intimidate the slave-hunters and their friends, and to prevent them from entering my house to search for slaves.

The pursuit was often very close, and we had to resort to various stratagems in order to elude the pursuers. Sometimes a company of fugitives were scattered, and secreted in the neighborhood until the hunters had given up the chase. At other times their route was changed and they were hurried forward with all speed. It was a continual excitement and anxiety to us, but the work was its own reward.

As I have said before, when we knew of no pursuit, and the fugitives needed to rest or to be clothed, or were sick from exposure and fatigue, we have kept them with us for weeks or months. A case of this kind was that of two young men who were brought to our house during a severe cold spell in the early part of winter. They had been out in the snow and ice, and their feet were so badly frozen that their boots had to be cut off, and they were compelled to lie by for three months, being unable to travel. Dr. Henry H. Way, who was always ready to minister to the fugitives, attended them, and by his skillful treatment their feet were saved, though for some time it was thought that a surgical operation would have to be performed. The two men left us in the spring, and went on to Canada. They seemed loth to part from us, and manifested much gratitude for our kindness and care. The next autumn one of them returned to our house to see us, saying that he felt so much indebted to us that he had come back to work for us to try to repay us, in some measure, for what we had done for him. I told him that we had no charge against him, and could not receive anything for our attention to him while he was sick and helpless; but if he thought he would be safe, I would hire him during the winter at good wages. He accepted this offer and proved to be a faithful servant. He attended night-school and made some progress in learning. He returned to Canada in the spring.

Many of the fugitives came long distances, from Alabama, Mississippi, Louisiana, in fact from all parts of the South. Sometimes the poor hunted creatures had been out so long, living in woods and thickets, that they were almost wild when they came in, and so fearful of being betrayed, that it was some time before their confidence could be gained and the true state of their case learned. Although the number of fugitives that I aided on their way was so large, not one, so far as I ever knew, was captured and taken back to slavery. Providence seemed to favor our efforts for the poor slaves, and to crown them with success.

INCIDENTS OF A TRIP TO NORTH CAROLINA

Early in the spring of 1828 I started to North Carolina on business for myself and others, taking with me a small drove of horses to sell.

I was accompanied by Ellis Mitchell, a light mulatto man, free born. He was from our neighborhood in North Carolina, where by his industry as a blacksmith he had become possessed of a comfortable little property adjoining the farm of my wife's father, Stanton White. In the fall of 1827 my father-in-law moved from North Carolina and settled in Spiceland, Henry County, Indiana. Ellis had long wished to pay a visit to the western country, but was deterred from making the attempt by a knowledge of the difficulties that beset a colored man, who traveled alone from a slave State to the free States. Therefore, when my father-in-law prepared to start, Ellis saw his opportunity. He offered his services to drive my father-in-law's team, and was gladly accepted.

He made the journey in safety and spent the winter in Indiana, visiting his numerous friends and acquaintances, who had emigrated from North Carolina. When he wished to return home in the spring, he offered to go with me and aid me in driving the horses, and I gladly availed myself of his services. Dr. Henry H. Way, who was then my partner in business, accompanied us on the first day's journey. We stopped at night at a tavern near Eaton, Ohio, had our horses put up and called for supper for three. When we were called to the supper table, however, we found plates and seats for only two. The doctor observed to the landlady that we had ordered supper for three, but that she had prepared for only two, and remarked: "Perhaps you did not understand that there were three in our company."

"Yes, sir," she replied; "I did understand, but we don't admit niggers to our table to eat with white folks. I will give your servant his supper in the kitchen."

"He is not our servant," rejoined the doctor; "but a respectable gentleman, fully as worthy as we are, and nearly as white; he owns good property, and is really worth more money than either of us."

"I don't care," she replied; "he can't eat at my table with white folks."

In his quaint, peculiar style of speaking the doctor asked: "Do you ever expect to go to heaven?"

"I hope so," she replied, wondering how such a question could refer to the subject of their conversation.

The doctor said: "If this man should go there, as I trust he will, do you think he will be put in the kitchen?" and then went on to quote several passages of Scripture, with which the woman was apparently not familiar, concluding by saying: "I had much rather eat with this man than with a person who would not eat with him."

But the landlady did not yield, and Ellis had to eat in the kitchen. We traveled through the State of Ohio, but had no further difficulty in regard to Ellis' accommodations until we crossed the river at Gallipolis and entered the State of Virginia. Then, Ellis was a "nigger" and had to go into the kitchen the most of the way. While traveling up the Kanawha River, there was a sudden change of temperature, and the weather, which had been mild and pleasant, became cold and blustering, and snow fell.

Ellis Mitchell became quite sick from exposure, and was hardly able to travel. We wished to stop early, but could find no house of entertainment. Some time after sunset we arrived at a good tavern and called for quarters. The landlord came out to meet us and appeared very accommodating. He called several negro servants to take our horses, and said to me: "Send your servant with mine to take care of the horses." I told him that I would go to the stable myself to look after the horses, as my companion was sick and I wished him to go in to the fire. I requested the landlord to give him a comfortable room where he could lie down, for he had had a hard ague chill in the afternoon and the fever was now coming on.

The landlord replied: "Oh yes, sir, he shall be properly attended to;" and I told Ellis to go in.

I went with the servants to see that our drove of horses was properly stabled and fed, then went back to the house and inquired about Ellis.

The landlord said: "My niggers will take care of him; don't be uneasy."

But I was determined to see where he was, and how he fared, and walking out of the back door, I proceeded to a negro cabin which I saw a few rods off. Entering it, I saw Ellis sitting on a rough bench in one corner, near a large fireplace in which burned a few sticks of wood. In the opposite corner sat several negro children on the dirt floor, for only half of the cabin, the back part, had a rough board floor. On these boards lay a few old blankets and quilts which afforded all the bed that Ellis could expect for the night.

I went back to the house with my feelings much disturbed, and said to the landlord: "I called for a comfortable room for the sick man, so that he might lie down, but I find him sitting on a rough bench, with no chance to lie down. I want him taken out of that dirty cabin and given a comfortable place to rest and sleep; he is able to pay for it. He is a free man, owning a good property, and at home has nice feather beds to sleep on."

The landlord replied: "I will see that he is made comfortable."

After supper, I went again to the cabin to see how Ellis was faring. I found him lying on the bench, with his overcoat over him. An old straw bed, with some ragged and dirty blankets, had been spread down in one corner for him, but he had refused to lie on it. For his supper he had been given some poor coffee and corn bread, of which he had tasted but little. The floor of the cabin was occupied by the negro servants, men, women, and children. Ellis spent the night on the bench by the fire, sleeping but little.

In the morning the breakfast offered him was the same as his supper, yet when we came to settle our accounts, his bill was the same as mine. Ellis had never been a slave, had always lived in a neighborhood of Friends, where he was respected and kindly treated, and this

was the first time he had experienced the effects of slavery. The rest of
the way home he fared more comfortably. After crossing the mountains into Patrick County, where taverns were few and far between, we
made an early start one morning, and traveled till ten o'clock to reach
an inn. We stopped and called for breakfast for two, and, after waiting
some time, I was informed that the meal was ready. I stepped into the
dining-room, but seeing only one plate on the table, I called to the
landlady, and said: "I ordered breakfast for two, and I wish this
gentleman to eat with me."

She replied: "After you have done, sir, he may come to the table."

I told her that we had no time to spare to eat, one after the other,
for we had a long journey before us that day, and wished to be off as
soon as possible.

"I don't care," she said, "niggers can't eat with white folks at my
table."

I answered: "That gentleman is nearly as white as I am, and is a
worthy man; I have no objections to eat with him."

She still persisted in her refusal; then I said: "I have no time to
parley. That man is older than I am; I will give him the preference if
either of us have to wait."

She at once set a plate on another table in the room, and set the
same fare before Ellis. So we were permitted to eat in the same room.

Ellis concluded that Virginia was a hard place for free negroes,
even if they happened to be nearly white, and was glad to get out of
the State, and reach his own comfortable home.

After spending a week in the neighborhood of my old home, and
disposing of part of my horses, I went farther south, into the edge of
South Carolina, on the Pedee River, thence turned my course toward
Fayetteville. Fifty miles south of that place lies the town of Lamber-
ton, where I arrived one day at noon, and stopped for dinner. I saw a
large crowd of people in the Court-House yard, and thought that it
would be a good opportunity to dispose of the few horses which I had
left. The landlord informed me that an auction was about to take
place—that a large number of slaves were to be sold that afternoon to
the highest bidders. As soon as dinner was over, I walked out to the
large lot in front of the Court-House, and looked about me. The

slaves who were to be sold stood in a group near the auctioneer's stand, which was a high platform with steps. They appeared intelligent, but their countenances betrayed deep dejection and anxiety. The men who intended to purchase passed from one to another of the group, examining them just as I would examine a horse which I wished to buy. These men seemed devoid of any feeling of humanity, and treated the negroes as if they were brutes. They examined their limbs and teeth to see if they were sound and healthy, and looked at their backs and heads, to see if they were scarred by whips, or other instruments of punishment. It was disgusting to witness their actions, and to hear their vulgar and profane language. Now and then one of them would make some obscene remark, and the rest would greet it with peals of laughter, but not a smile passed over the sad countenances of the slaves. There were men, women and children to be sold, the adults appearing to be in the prime of life. When the examination was over, the auctioneer mounted the platform, taking one of the slave men with him. He described the good qualities of that valuable piece of property,—then the bidding commenced. The slave looked anxiously and eagerly from one bidder to another, as if trying to read in their countenances their qualities as masters, and his fate. The crier's hammer soon came down, then another slave was placed upon the stand, and bid off. After several men had been sold in this way, a woman was placed upon the stand, with a child in her arms apparently a year old. She was a fine looking woman, in the prime of life, with an intelligent countenance, clouded with the deepest sadness. The auctioneer recommended her as a good cook, house servant, and field hand—indeed, according to his representation, she could turn her hand to anything, and was an unusually valuable piece of property. She was industrious, honest and trustworthy, and, above all, she was a Christian, a member of the church—as if the grace of God would add to her price! The bidding was quite lively, and she sold for a high price. I supposed that the child was included in the sale, of course, but soon saw that it was to be sold separately. The mother begged her new master to buy her child, but he did not want it, and would not listen to her pleading.

The child was sold to another man, but when he came to take it from her, she clasped her arms around it tighter than ever and clung to it. Her master came up and tore it from her arms amid her piercing shrieks and cries, and dragged her away, cursing and abusing her as he went. The scene moved my heart to its depths; I could endure it no longer. I left the ground, returned to my tavern, called for my horses, and left the town without attempting to do any business. As I mounted my horse, I heard the voice of the slave mother as she screamed: "My child, my child!" I rode away as fast as I could, to get beyond the sound of her cries. But that night I could not sleep; her screams rang in my ears, and haunted me for weeks afterward.

This incident increased my abhorrence of slavery and strengthened my determination to labor for the cruelly oppressed slaves. I resolved to labor in this cause until the end of my days, not expecting that I would live to see the fetters broken and the bondmen free, yet hoping that the time of redemption was not far distant. I returned home with feelings of renewed energy and zeal for the cause of liberty.

I devoted much time and labor to aiding the poor fugitives, but found opportunity to engage in other benevolent work. The Society of Friends had a standing committee, called the "Committee on the Concerns of the People of Color," whose business it was to look after the educational interest of the free colored people among us. I was a member of that committee. A fund was raised every year by our society to sustain schools, and to aid the poor and destitute among the colored people. I was appointed treasurer of this fund. We had several large settlements of free colored people in the limits of our Quarterly Meeting, which were under our care, and we sustained schools among them. . . .

III.

Newport Stories—The Cunning Slave—
Robert Burrel—Eliza Harris—
Sam, the Eloquent Slave . . .
A Slave-hunter Outwitted

⊂Ε Of the many hundred cases that came under our personal notice during the twenty years that we lived at Newport, Indiana, a few
will be given. I shall not attempt to give dates, nor the names of the
runaway slaves. When the fugitives came to our house, they seldom
gave the name by which they had been known in slavery, or if they
did, we gave them another name, by which they were afterward
known both at our house and in Canada. The stories that follow are
gathered from the slaves' own narratives.

THE CUNNING SLAVE

Jim was a shrewd, intelligent chattel, the property of a man living in
Kentucky. Having in some unaccountable manner got the idea that
freedom was better than bondage, he resolved to make an effort to
gain his liberty. He did not make his intention known to his wife or
any of his fellow-bondmen, choosing to make the attempt alone. He
watched for an opportunity to escape, and when it came he started for
the Ohio River. He knew that he was a valuable piece of property, and
that his master would pursue him and make strong efforts to capture
him, so he let no grass grow under his feet till he reached the bank of
the river. He wandered along this in the dark for some time, looking

for a way to cross, and finally came to the hut of a colored man. He told his story to the negro living in the hut, and offered him part of the small sum of money he had if he would take him across in a skiff to the Indiana shore. The negro knew where a skiff lay drawn up on the shore, and consented to row him across. Jim reached the other side safely, and landed a short distance above Madison. It was now near daylight, and he must hasten to seek a place of concealment. He was directed how to find George De Baptist, a free colored man, who often aided fugitive slaves. George then lived in Madison, but soon after removed to Detroit, Michigan, for his own safety. Jim made his way to the house of this friendly colored man, and remained secreted during the day. Some time in the day, George De Baptist learned that Jim's master had arrived in town with a posse of men, and that they were rudely entering the houses of colored people, searching for the missing slave. By shrewd management on the part of George, the hunters were baffled, and the next night Jim was conducted through corn-fields and by-ways to a depot of the Underground Railroad. He was forwarded from station to station, at late hours in the night, until he reached William Beard's, in Union County, Indiana. Here he rested a few days, under the roof of that noted and worthy abolitionist, whose house was known for many years as a safe retreat for the oppressed fugitive. From that place he was conducted to our house, a distance of about twenty-five miles, and, after remaining with us one day, he was forwarded on from station to station, till he reached Canada. Here he remained a few months. In telling his story, he said:

"Oh, how sweet it was to breathe free air, to feel that I had no massa who could whip me or sell me. But I was not happy long. I could not enjoy liberty when the thoughts of my poor wife and children in slavery would rise up before me. I thought to myself, I have learned the way and found friends all along the road; now I will go back and fetch my wife and children. I'll go to old massa's plantation, and I'll make believe I am tired of freedom. I'll tell old massa a story that will please him; then I will go to work hard and watch for a chance to slip away my wife and children."

So Jim left Canada and wended his way back to the old plantation in Kentucky. His master was greatly surprised, one morning, to see his missing property come walking up from the negro quarters as if nothing had happened. Jim came up to him and made a low bow, and stood before him as humble as a whipped dog. In answer to the volley of questions and hard names that greeted him, Jim said:

"I thought I wanted to be free, massa, so I run away and went to Canada. But I had a hard time there, and soon got tired of taking care of myself. I thought I would rather live with massa again and be a good servant. I found that Canada was no place for niggers; it's too cold, and we can't make any money there. Mean white folks cheat poor niggers out of their wages when they hire them. I soon got sick of being free, and wished I was back on the old plantation. And those people called abolitionists, that I met with on the way, are a mean set of rascals. They pretend to help the niggers, but they cheat them all they can. They get all the work out of a nigger they can, and never pay him for it. I tell you, massa, they are mean folks."

In narrating his story, Jim said: "Well, old massa seemed mightily pleased with my lies. He spoke pleasant to me, and said: 'Jim, I hope you will make a good missionary among our people and the neighbors.' I got massa's confidence, and worked well and obeyed him well, and I talked to the niggers before him, in a way to please him. But they could understand me, for I had been doing missionary work among them, and the neighbors' niggers too, but not such missionary work as massa thought I was doing."

Jim worked on faithfully through the fall and winter months, all the time arranging matters for a second flight.

In the spring, when the weather was warm, he succeeded in getting his wife and children and a few of his slave friends across the Ohio River into Indiana. He got safely to the first station of the Underground Railroad, with his party, numbering fourteen, and hurried on with them rapidly from station to station, until they reached our house. They were hotly pursued and had several narrow escapes, but the wise management of their friends on the route prevented them from being captured. They remained at our house several days to rest, as they were much exhausted with night travel, and suffering from exposure, and while they were concealed in our garret, their pursuers passed through the town.

The hunters went northward by way of Winchester and Cabin Creek, where there was a large settlement of free colored people. While they were searching in these neighborhoods, we forwarded the fugitives on another route, by way of Spartansburg, Greenville and Mercer County, Ohio, to Sandusky. From this place they were shipped across the lake to Fort Malden, Canada. Jim's opinions, as he had expressed them to his master, now underwent a sudden change. He liked the country and the people, and thought that he could make a living not only for himself, but for his family. As to the abolitionists along the route, he thought they were the best people in the world. Instead of cheating the poor fugitives by getting their services without pay, they fed and clothed them without charge, and would help them on their journey; often using their own horses and wagons, and traveling all night with the fugitives. A few years after I had the pleasure of seeing Jim and his family in their comfortable home in Canada. Jim said he hoped God would forgive him for telling his master so many lies. He said he felt no feelings of homesickness, no longings for massa and the old plantation in Kentucky.

ROBERT BURREL

A colored man, who gave his name as Robert Burrel, came to my house, seeking employment. He said he had been working several months at Flat Rock, in Henry County, but that his employer there had no work for him during the winter, and had recommended him to call on me. He said he had been brought up in Tennessee, but, thinking he had rather live in a free State, had come to Indiana a few months before. I liked his sober and intelligent appearance, and gave him employment in my pork-house. I found him to be a deeply religious man and a most faithful and trustworthy servant. He was pleasant in his manner and speech, but was never heard to indulge in loud laughter. He seemed to have some serious subject on his mind, over which he was constantly brooding. If any one inquired particularly concerning his past life, he evaded the questions, and it was not until he had been in my employment for several months that he ventured to tell me the true state of his case. He was a runaway slave, and belonged to a man living in East Tennessee. He had married a free colored woman living there, and was as happy as it was possible for a slave to be, until he learned that his master was about to sell him to a trader who would take him to the far South. Then he ran away, leaving his wife and two children, and made his way to Indiana. His object was to gain enough money to buy his freedom and send for his family. He had been working with this end in view, but had kept his fears, hopes and anxieties in his own heart, lest he should be betrayed and lose the liberty that was so sweet. His story gained my sympathy, and I promised to aid him in any way I could. We often consulted together concerning his wife and two little boys. He represented his wife as being a Christian woman, and said that she was a member of the Methodist Church; to which he also belonged. She had promised to remain faithful to him, and to await patiently the result of his effort. I discouraged his attempt to buy himself, as it would take several years of hard work, and might then be a failure. I advised him to save all the money he could, and perhaps some way would open by which his wife and children could get to him, and go with him to Canada. But he felt very timid about sending for his wife and children before securing his own freedom, for he feared they would be tracked and his whereabouts discovered.

I continued him in my employ, putting him in my linseed oil mill, and paying him extra wages for his care and good management. In conversation with him, one day, I found that he knew something about John Rankin, a noted abolitionist and Presbyterian clergyman, formerly of East Tennessee, but then living at Ripley, Ohio.

I wrote to friend Rankin, giving the outlines of Robert's story, and asking him if he thought the wife and two children could be brought to Ohio without arousing the suspicions of Robert's master and leading to his detection. He wrote me, in reply, that some of his family were going to East Tennessee soon, on a visit to their relatives there, and he thought they could have an interview with Robert's wife, and arrange to have her and the children removed to Ohio. I kept up a correspondence with him on the subject, and ascertaining that it would cost about forty dollars to move the woman and children to Ohio, I sent him that amount, to be applied for that purpose. I sent a message to be delivered to Robert's wife, telling her that if she would come to Ripley, Ohio, she could gain information of her husband. The message was delivered to her by the friends of John Rankin, but they did not succeed in gaining her confidence, and she would not come to Ohio, fearing that it was a scheme to betray her husband. So the project failed at that time, and John Rankin returned the money I had sent him; but two years later we renewed our efforts, and succeeded in bringing the woman and her children to Ripley. From this place, lest somebody should have traced them from Tennessee, hoping to learn the whereabouts of Robert, they were taken to Cincinnati. Soon afterward they were brought to my house in Newport, and there was a joyful meeting between husband and wife, after a separation of four years.

I purchased for them a little home in Newport, which Robert paid for by his work, and here they lived happily several years, with none to molest or make them afraid. When the fugitive slave law of 1850 was passed, they left and went to Canada for greater security.

THE STORY OF ELIZA HARRIS

Eliza Harris, of "Uncle Tom's Cabin" notoriety, the slave woman who crossed the Ohio River, near Ripley, on the drifting ice with her child in her arms, was sheltered under our roof and fed at our table for several days. This was while we lived at Newport, Indiana, which is six miles west of the State line of Ohio. To elude the pursuers who were following closely on her track, she was sent across to our line of the Underground Railroad.

The story of this slave woman, so graphically told by Harriet Beecher Stowe in "Uncle Tom's Cabin," will, no doubt, be remembered by every reader of that deeply interesting book. The cruelties of slavery depicted in that remarkable work are not overdrawn. The stories are founded on facts that really occurred, real names being wisely withheld, and fictitious names and imaginary conversations often inserted. From the fact that Eliza Harris was sheltered at our house several days, it was generally believed among those acquainted with the circumstances that I and my wife were the veritable Simeon and Rachel Halliday, the Quaker couple alluded to in "Uncle Tom's Cabin." I will give a short sketch of the fugitive's story, as she related it.

She said she was a slave from Kentucky, the property of a man who lived a few miles back from the Ohio River, below Ripley, Ohio. Her master and mistress were kind to her, and she had a comfortable home, but her master got into some pecuniary difficulty, and she found that she and her only child were to be separated. She had buried two children, and was doubly attached to the one she had left, a bright, promising child, over two years old. When she found that it was to be taken from her, she was filled with grief and dismay, and resolved to make her escape that night if possible. She watched her opportunity, and when darkness had settled down and all the family had retired to sleep, she started with her child in her arms and walked straight toward the Ohio River. She knew that it was frozen over, at that season of the year, and hoped to cross without difficulty on the ice, but when she reached its banks at daylight, she found that the ice had broken up and was slowly drifting in large cakes. She ventured to go to a house near by, where she was kindly received and permitted to remain through the day. She hoped to find some way to cross the river the next night, but there seemed little prospect of any one being able to cross in safety, for during the day the ice became more broken and dangerous to cross. In the evening she discovered pursuers nearing the house, and with desperate courage she determined to cross the river, or perish in the attempt. Clasping her child in her arms she darted out of the back door and ran toward the river, followed by her pursuers, who had just dismounted from their horses when they caught sight of her. No fear or thought of personal danger entered Eliza's mind, for she felt that she had rather be drowned than to be captured and separated from her child. Clasping her babe to her bosom with her left arm, she sprang on to the first cake of ice, then from that to another and another. Some times the cake she was on would sink beneath her weight, then she would slide her child on to the next cake, pull herself on with her hands, and so continue her hazardous journey. She became wet to the waist with ice water and her hands were benumbed with cold, but as she made her way from one cake of ice to another, she felt that surely the Lord was preserving and upholding her, and that nothing could harm her.

When she reached the Ohio side, near Ripley, she was completely exhausted and almost breathless. A man, who had been standing on the bank watching her progress with amazement and expecting every moment to see her go down, assisted her up the bank. After she had recovered her strength a little he directed her to a house on the hill, in the outskirts of town. She made her way to the place, and was kindly received and cared for. It was not considered safe for her to remain there during the night, so, after resting a while and being provided with food and dry clothing, she was conducted to a station on the Underground Railroad, a few miles farther from the river. The next night she was forwarded on from station to station to our house in Newport, where she arrived safely and remained several days.

Other fugitives arrived in the meantime, and Eliza and her child were sent with them, by the Greenville branch of the Underground Railroad, to Sandusky, Ohio. They reached that place in safety, and crossed the lake to Canada, locating finally at Chatham, Canada West.

In the summer of 1854 I was on a visit to Canada, accompanied by my wife and daughter, and Laura S. Haviland, of Michigan. At the close of a meeting which we attended, at one of the colored churches, a woman came up to my wife, seized her hand, and exclaimed: "How are you, Aunt Katie? God bless you!" etc. My wife did not recognize her, but she soon called herself to our remembrance by referring to the time she was at our house in the days of her distress, when my wife gave her the name of Eliza Harris, and by relating other particulars. We visited her at her house while at Chatham, and found her comfortable and contented.

Many other fugitives came and spoke to us, whom we did not recognize or remember until they related some incident that recalled them to mind. Such circumstances occurred in nearly every neighborhood we visited in Canada. Hundreds who had been sheltered under our roof and fed at our table, when fleeing from the land of whips and chains, introduced themselves to us and referred to the time, often fifteen or twenty years before, when we had aided them.

On the first day of August, 1854, we went, with a large company from Windsor, to attend a celebration of the West India emancipation. The meeting was held in a dense settlement of fugitives, about eight miles south of Windsor. Several public speakers from Detroit were in our party. A platform had been erected in a grove near the school-house, where Laura S. Haviland had established a school for fugitives. The day was fine, and there was a large crowd of colored people, who had come from various settlements to hear the speaking. Here we met quite a number of those whom we had helped on their way to freedom, and the gratitude they expressed was quite affecting. One old white-headed man came to my wife, and said he wanted to get hold of her hand. She reached her hand to him, and while he held it, he said: "Don't you 'member me, Misses?"

She looked at him closely, and said: "No, I believe I do not remember thee."

Then the old negro said: "La me! Misses, don't you 'member when dey was close after me to take me an' you hid me in de feather bed and saved me? Why, bress your heart! if it hadn't been for you I should nebber been here. It's more dan twenty years ago, and my head is white, but I hasn't forgot dat time."

She shook his hand heartily, and said: "Now I remember thee."

At Amherstburg, generally called Fort Malden, and many other places, we met with many, both men and women, whom we had assisted on their way to liberty, and their expressions of thankfulness and regard were very gratifying to us.

SAM, THE ELOQUENT SLAVE

The subject of this sketch was the property of a man living near Lexington, Kentucky. He had a wife and several children whom he was permitted to visit frequently, was well treated by his master, and had no fear of being sold away from his family; so his condition was a very favorable one, compared with that of many other slaves. But this state of security came suddenly to an end. The master died and the heirs decided to sell Sam, but as he was very powerful, and a dangerous man to deal with when his spirit was roused, no one dared to take possession of him and tell him that he was sold away from his family.

What could not be done by force was accomplished by stratagem. Sam was sent into the jail to take a box of candles, and, all unsuspecting, walked into the trap. Several men were hidden behind the door, and leaping out suddenly, they knocked him down, overpowered and bound him. He then learned that he was bought by a negro trader, who intended taking him to the South. Just before the coffle started, Sam's wife was permitted to come to the jail to bid him good-bye, but her distress was so great and she wept so loudly that she was hurried out and taken away without having been able to say a word. Sam was taken to Mississippi and sold, but after several months managed to escape, and after much difficulty and many hardships found his way back to Lexington, Kentucky, where he hoped to find some one who would purchase him and allow him to remain near his family, but in this effort he did not succeed.

Hearing that pursuers were on his track, he left that neighborhood, and succeeded in making his way to Newport, Indiana, where he arrived in the dead of winter, in a destitute and suffering condition.

I persuaded him to remain till better weather, when the roads would be open and traveling easier, and he remained till spring, I in the meantime furnishing him with employment at good wages. It may be in place here to mention that the abolitionists were frequently accused, by pro-slavery people, of availing themselves of the labor of the fugitive slaves by employing them several months on the promise of good wages, then raising the alarm that the masters were in pursuit, and hustling them off on the road to Canada without paying the wages due them. It is almost needless to say that this accusation was false. During that winter there was a monthly prayer-meeting, held in the Wesleyan Chapel at Newport, on behalf of the slaves, and I asked Sam to attend one of these meetings with me. He at first hesitated, so fearful was he of being betrayed, but on being assured that there was no danger, he consented to go.

It seemed strange to him that white people should pray for slaves; he had never heard of such a thing before. As others were telling stories of the sufferings of slaves, I suggested to Sam that he should give his experience. To this he consented, with reluctance, and I rose and informed the meeting that a fugitive slave was sitting by my side, whose story I was sure would be interesting to all present. Sam then rose from his seat and gave a short history of his sufferings, together with a vivid description of the horrors of slavery, and so interested his hearers that they expressed a desire to hear him again.

He was prevailed upon to speak another time, when a larger number would have an opportunity to hear him, and a meeting was appointed for this purpose. When the evening came the church was crowded. Sam was conducted to the pulpit by the minister and myself. We made short introductory speeches, then Sam spoke for more than an hour to the attentive and deeply interested audience. They had not expected to hear good language from a slave who had had no educational advantages, and were surprised to find his speech resembling that of a practiced orator. Sam had, during the life of his indulgent master, had frequent opportunities of hearing public speeches in Lexington, and this experience, which had been a sort of education to him, added to his native eloquence, enabled him to hold his audience spellbound, while he depicted in glowing words the cruelty of slavery and the manifold sufferings of the slaves. He then gave an account of his own trials, and pictured in a touching manner the scene of his wife's separation from him when he was bound in jail, and finished with an appeal to the audience so full of pathos that the heart of every one was touched, and nearly all his hearers were melted to tears.

Some of them declared afterward that they thought Henry Clay could not surpass him in eloquence. Shortly after this the United Brethren held a Conference in Newport, and wishing to have Sam address them, a deputation called at my house, to speak with him on the subject. They were shown into the parlor, where a fire was burning, and as I sat talking with them, Sam came in with an armful of wood to replenish the fire.

One of the deputation said: "Is this the man?" and I answered, "Yes;" then remarked to Sam that these men wished to see him. Sam went out quickly and did not return. When I went to look for him, I found him outside the kitchen door, with a large butcher knife in his hand, ready to defend himself. He thought that the men had come to take him, and was determined to sell his life or liberty as dearly as possible. When the matter was explained, he went in to see the men, and afterward spoke for them. In the spring he was sent on to Canada, where he was out of the slave-dealer's power forever. . . .

A SLAVE-HUNTER OUTWITTED

The story that I am about to relate may, in some of its particulars, seem improbable or even impossible, to any reader not acquainted with the workings of the southern division of the Underground Railroad. That two young slave girls could successfully make their escape from a Southern State and travel hundreds of miles, hiding in the day, in thickets and other secluded places, and traveling at night, crossing rivers and swamps, and passing undiscovered through settlements, appears more like a story of romance than one of sober reality. But I will not test the reader's credulity by leaving this story unexplained; I will give a few items regarding the manner of the escape of many slaves from the South. I have always contended that the Underground Railroad, so called, was a Southern institution; that it had its origin in the slave States. It was, however, conducted on quite a different principle south of Mason and Dixon's line, from what it was on this side. South of the line money, in most cases, was the motive; north, we generally worked on principle. For the sake of money, people in the South would help slaves to escape and convey them across the line, and by this means, women with their children, and young girls, like the subjects of this story, were enabled to reach the North. They were hidden in wagons, or stowed away in secret places on steamboats, or conducted on foot through the country, by shrewd managers who traveled at night and knew what places to avoid.

Free colored people who had relatives in slavery were willing to contribute to the utmost of their means, to aid in getting their loved ones out of bondage; just as we would do if any of our loved ones were held in thralldom. It was by some line of the Southern Underground Railroad that two slave girls, living in Tennessee, managed to escape and reach Cabin Creek, Randolph County, Indiana, where lived their grandparents and most of their near relatives, who were free.

This neighborhood was settled principally by free colored people who had purchased government land in forty or eighty acre lots; in some instances a quarter section—one hundred and sixty acres—had been entered. A dense settlement of free colored people had formed at Cabin Creek, and a good school had been established there, under the auspices of New Garden Quarterly Meeting of Friends.

Near the center of the colony lived the grandparents of the two girls mentioned, and there the girls staid, after their long and perilous journey, enjoying their newly gained liberty, and hoping that their master would never learn of their whereabouts. But they were not destined to dwell here in safety. Their master had come to Richmond, ostensibly to look about the neighborhood and buy cattle, but really to gain some trace of his slave property. He hired spies and sent them into different neighborhoods, Cabin Creek among the rest, and thus the girls were discovered. When the master learned that his two slave girls were so near, he felt as if they were already in his power, but when he heard more concerning Cabin Creek neighborhood and the character of the colored people there, he began to think it might not be so easy to effect a capture. When a slave-hunter came to Cabin Creek, the people banded together to protect the fugitive he was after, and as they were very determined in their defense it was a difficult matter to capture the slave. They had prearranged signals for such occasions, and the alarm soon called the people together.

The master of the two girls obtained a writ and placed it in the hands of an officer, then gathered a company of roughs from Richmond, Winchester and other neighborhoods, and rode out to Cabin Creek at the head of a large company of armed men. They marched to the cabin where the two girls were, and surrounded it.

The alarm was given as soon as the company were seen approaching, and a boy mounted a horse and rode off at full speed to spread the alarm. He was fired at by some of the company, and a rifle ball grazed his arm, making a slight flesh wound. This only hastened his speed and increased the excitement. The grandfather of the two girls was away from home, but the brave old grandmother seized a corn-cutter and placed herself in the only door of the cabin, defying the crowd and declaring that she would cut the first man in two who undertook to cross the threshold. Thus she kept the slave-hunter and his posse at bay, while a large crowd of colored people collected. Quite a number of white people came also, some out of curiosity or sympathy with the master, and others who sympathized with the fugitives. It is said that there were more than two hundred people gathered around the cabin. The sound of the horn, and the message of the boy, had brought together most of the colored people in the settlement. An uncle of the slave girls, who lived near by, seeing the crowd as they rode up, placed himself near his mother, on the outside of the door, and several other sturdy negroes stood by his side.

He was a shrewd sharp fellow, with a fair education, and kept his presence of mind under the exciting circumstances. He demanded to see the writ, and it was handed to him by the officer. He read it over carefully, and tried to pick flaws in it. He denied that it gave them any authority to enter that house to search for property. The laws of Indiana did not recognize human beings as property until they had been proven to be such, and that was a difficult thing to do. He said that he doubted very much whether the man who had obtained this writ to arrest two slave girls could prove them to be his property. Furthermore, he did not believe the girls were in that house. He extended the debate with the master as long as possible, and in the meantime several colored people had been permitted to pass in and out under the sharp edge of the old woman's corn-cutter, but no white person had been admitted.

While the debate was going on, arrangements were being made, both outdoors and indoors, for the escape of the girls. The uncle understood all this perfectly, and he was doing his part toward success, by prolonging the palaver. The girls dressed in boys' clothes, and put on slouch hats; then, while the debate outside grew warm and excitement began to run high, and the slave-hunters to declare that they would enter the house, in spite of the corn-cutter and other obstructions, the girls passed out of the door with other negroes, and made their way through the crowd. Two fleet horses, with light but very capable riders, stood near the side of a large log, screened from the sight of the crowd by some tall bushes. The girls stepped quickly on the log and sprang, one on each horse, behind the riders, and were soon out of sight. When the uncle knew that the girls were at a safe distance, he began to moderate and proposed a compromise. Speaking in a whisper to his mother, he appeared to be consulting with her on the subject, and finally said, that if the master of the girls would agree to give them a fair trial at Winchester, he and his posse would be allowed to enter the house peaceably. This was agreed to, and the grandmother laid aside her weapon of defense, and appeared calm and subdued. The master and his posse rushed in to seize the girls, and those outside, who could not see into the house, listened to hear the girls' screams of terror and pleadings for mercy while their master bound them. But they heard nothing of the kind, only oaths and exclamations from the men as they searched about the cabin and up in the loft. The hunters were baffled; the girls were not to be found. The darkies seemed in a good humor, and there was a general display of white teeth in broad grins. Some of the white folks also seemed amused, and inclined to make sport of the misfortune of the master. It was no laughable matter to him—to be duped by negroes and to lose such valuable property as these girls were, either of whom would soon be worth one thousand dollars. Some in the crowd were unfeeling enough to jest at his loss, and to advise him to look around and see if there was not a hole in the ground where the girls had been let down to the Underground Railroad.

When the master fully realized how he had been outwitted, his wrath knew no bounds, but his hired assistants tried to comfort him with the thought that they could soon ferret out the fugitives, and promised to make a thorough search through all the abolition neighborhoods.

The girls were taken a short distance on the Winchester road; then through by-ways and cross-roads they were brought through the Cherry Grove settlement of Friends to Newport, a distance of about twenty miles. The girls were much exhausted when they arrived at our house, having had a hard ride, part of the way in the night. After taking some nourishment, they were placed in a private room to rest during the remainder of the night, and were soon sound asleep. We did not apprehend any danger that night, as we supposed a vigorous search would be made at Cabin Creek and neighboring settlements, and that our town would not be searched till the hunt in the other localities had been prosecuted and proved fruitless.

Some time the next day, a messenger arrived at my house from Cabin Creek, and told us that after failing to find the girls at their grandfather's, the posse of pursuers had divided into several squads to search the different neighborhoods, and that one company were on their way to Newport. That afternoon several strangers were seen rambling about our village, inquiring for stray horses, and going abruptly into the houses of colored people living in the suburbs. It was not difficult to guess what was their real business. I was busy in my store when I learned of the conduct of these strangers, but went at once to the house and told my wife that negro hunters were in town, and that she must secrete the two girls. She was used to such business, and was not long in devising a plan. Taking the two girls, who had by this time been dressed in female apparel, into a bedroom, she hid them between the straw tick and feather tick, allowing them room for breathing, then made up the bed as usual, smoothed the counterpane and put on the pillows. But the girls were so excited and amused at the remembrance of how they outwitted massa, and of their ride, dressed in boys' clothes, and at their novel position, that they laughed and giggled until my wife had to separate them, and put one in another bed. I went back to my store and left Aunt Katy, as every one called my wife, to manage affairs at the house. If the searchers attempted to enter our house, she was to rattle the large dinner bell violently, and at this signal the neighbors would rush in, and I would get the proper officers and have the negro hunters arrested for attempting to enter my house without legal authority.

But these proceedings were not necessary. The hunters did not have courage enough to enter my house, though they knew it was a depot of the Underground Railroad. Hearing that threats were made against them in the village, they left without giving us any trouble.

We kept the girls very secluded for several weeks until the master had given up the search, and gone home. Then having other fugitives to forward to the North, we sent them altogether *via* the Greenville and Sandusky route to Canada, where they arrived in safety.

IV.

First Visit to Canada in 1844

⊂⊋ In the fall of 1844, William Beard, of Union County, Indiana, a minister of the religious Society of Friends, felt a concern to visit, in gospel love, the fugitive slaves who had escaped from Southern bondage and settled in Canada. A number of them had stopped at his house in their flight, and had been forwarded by him to my house, a distance of thirty miles. He felt that I was the person who should accompany him on this mission, and came to see me to present the subject. I heartily united with him, having felt a similar desire. We then laid the concern before our different Monthly Meetings, where it was cordially united with, and a certificate of unity and concurrence was given us. Thus provided with the proper credentials, and with the love of God in our hearts, we set out on our mission to the poor fugitives, intending also to visit the missionary stations among the Indians in Canada.

We started on horseback on the sixteenth day of the ninth month—September. On our way we visited several colored settlements in Ohio and Michigan, and held meetings with the people.

We reached Detroit on the twenty-fifth of the ninth month, about noon, and in company with Dr. Porter, a noted abolitionist of that city, spent the afternoon visiting the colored schools and various families of fugitives, many of whom remembered us, having stopped at our houses on their way from slavery to freedom. In the evening we attended a good meeting among the colored people. . . .

On the twenty-sixth we passed over to Windsor, on the Canada side. Here, and at Sandwich, we visited a number of colored families,

[73]

many of whom recognized me at once, having been at my house in the days of their distress when fleeing from a land of whips and chains.

The Queen's Court was in session at Sandwich while we were there, and a white man was on trial for having, under the inducement of a bribe, decoyed a fugitive across the river into the hands of his master. We went into court and listened for a time with much interest to the lawyers pleading. We heard Colonel Prince reaffirm the proud boast of England, that the moment a fugitive set his foot on British soil his shackles fell off and he was free. We afterward learned that a heavy penalty of fine and imprisonment was placed on the culprit.

From Sandwich we made our way down the Canada side of the Detroit River to Amherstburg, generally called Fort Malden, near the head of Lake Erie. In this old military town, and in the vicinity, a great many fugitives had located. The best tavern, or house of public entertainment, in the town, was kept by William Hamilton, a colored man. While at this place we made our headquarters at Isaac J. Rice's missionary buildings, where he had a large school for colored children. He had labored here among the colored people, mostly fugitives, for six years. He was a devoted self-denying worker, had received very little pecuniary help, and had suffered many privations. He was well situated in Ohio, as pastor of a Presbyterian church, and had fine prospects before him, but believed that the Lord called him to this field of missionary labor among the fugitive slaves who came here by hundreds and by thousands, poor, destitute and ignorant, suffering from all the evil influences of slavery. We entered into deep sympathy with him in his labors, realizing the great need there was here for just such an institution as he had established. He had sheltered at this missionary home many hundreds of fugitives till other homes for them could be found. This was the great landing point, the principal terminus of the Underground Railroad of the West.

We held meetings among the fugitives here and in the various settlements in the neighborhood. Isaac J. Rice accompanied us on these visits, and down the lake to Colchester and Gosfield. Here we had several meetings and visited many families, hearing thrilling stories of their narrow escapes, their great sufferings and the remarkable providences that attended their efforts to gain freedom. They told how they had prayed to the Lord, asking him to be with them and protect them in their flight from their tyrannical masters, and how he had never forsaken them in their time of need, but had fulfilled his promise to go with them. They frequently spoke as if they had held personal conversations with the Lord, and their simple and untutored language was full of expression of praise and thanksgiving. I was often led to believe that these poor ignorant and degraded sons and daughters of Africa, who were not able to read the words of the precious Savior, were blessed with a clearer, plainer manifestation of the Holy Spirit than many of us who have had better opportunities of cultivation. My heart was often touched and my eyes filled with tears on hearing their simple stories, or listening to their fervent earnest prayers in the services of family devotion, which we held from house to house. Holding meetings in families and in public constituted our work among them. We visited all the principal settlements of fugitives in Canada West, as well as the various missionary stations among the tribes of Indians there, and had an interesting and satisfactory season among them. We spent nearly two months in this way, traveling from place to place on horseback, as there were no railroads in that section then.

Leaving Gosfield County we made our way to Chatham and Sydenham, visiting the various neighborhoods of colored people. We spent several days at the settlement near Down's Mills, and visited the institution under the care of Hiram Wilson, called the British and American Manual Labor Institute for Colored Children. Friends in England had furnished the money to purchase the land and aid in establishing the institution; Friends of New York Yearly Meeting also contributed to aid this work. The school was then in a prosperous condition.

From this place we proceeded up the river Thames to London, visiting the different settlements of colored people on our way, and then went to the Wilberforce Colony. This was the only settlement we visited in our travels where we did not find fugitives who had been sheltered under my roof and fed at my table during their flight from bondage.

At the close of our religious meetings I generally addressed the colored people on the subject of education. I urged the parents to

send their children to school, and to attend Sabbath-schools and
night-schools themselves whenever opportunity offered; to learn at
least to read the Bible. We had visited most of their schools, and I
contrasted their present situation and advantages with their former
state of servitude, where they were not allowed to learn to read. I
sometimes mentioned that I had had the privilege of aiding some of
them in the time of their distress, of sheltering them under my roof
and feeding them at my table when they were fleeing from the hardships and cruelties of slavery and seeking safety and freedom in the
Queen's dominions. Whenever I touched that subject it brought out
shouts of "Bless the Lord! I know you. If it hadn't been for you I
wouldn't be here;" and at the close of the meeting the people would
come round us to shake hands in such crowds that it was impossible
for all to get hold of our hands. Some would cling to our garments as
if they thought they would impart some virtue. I often met fugitives
who had been at my house ten or fifteen years before, so long ago that
I had forgotten them, and could recall no recollection of them until
they mentioned some circumstance that brought them to mind. Some
of them were well situated, owned good farms, and were perhaps
worth more than their former masters. Land had been easily obtained
and many had availed themselves of this advantage to secure comfortable homesteads. Government land had been divided up into fifty-
acre lots, which they could buy for two dollars an acre, and have ten
years in which to pay for it, and if it was not paid for at the end of that
time they did not lose all the labor they had bestowed on it, but received a clear title to the land as soon as they paid for it.

We found many of the fugitives more comfortably situated than
we expected, but there was much destitution and suffering among
those who had recently come in. Many fugitives arrived weary and
footsore, with their clothing in rags, having been torn by briers and
bitten by dogs on their way, and when the precious boon of freedom
was obtained, they found themselves possessed of little else, in a country unknown to them and a climate much colder than that to which
they were accustomed.

We noted the cases and localities of destitution, and after our return home took measures to collect and forward several large boxes of

clothing and bedding to be distributed by reliable agents to the most needy. Numbers arrived every week on the different lines of the Underground Railroad, destitute of every comfort and almost of clothing; so we found that end of our road required Christian care and benevolence as well as this. We were gratified to learn that the colored people of Canada had organized benevolent associations among themselves, for the purpose of assisting the newly arrived fugitives as far as they could. . . .

V.

John Fairfield, the Southern Abolitionist

☙ It is seldom that one hears of a person who has been brought up in the midst of slavery, surrounded by its influences from his earliest recollection, being a hater of the "peculiar institution," but there are several such cases on record. . . .

His early home was in Virginia, east of the mountains, where he imbibed anti-slavery sentiments—from what source it is unknown, certainly not from his relatives, who were all slaveholders. When quite a young man, he decided to make a visit to the State of Ohio, and seek his fortunes in a free State. Thinking that it would be a good opportunity to put his anti-slavery principles into practice, he planned to take with him one of his uncle's slaves, a bright, intelligent young man, about his own age, to whom he was much attached. John and this young colored man had played together when boys, and had been brought up together. They had often discussed plans by which Bill, the slave, could make his escape to Canada, but no attempt had been made to carry them out, until young Fairfield determined to visit Ohio. The arrangement was then made for Bill to take one of his master's horses, and make his escape the night before Fairfield started, and wait for him at a rendezvous appointed. This plan was carried out, and Bill traveled as Fairfield's servant until they reached Ohio. Not feeling safe in that State, he went on to Canada, accompanied by Fairfield, who spent several weeks there looking at the country. Bill, in the meanwhile, found a good situation, and when Fairfield left him he was rejoicing in his newly achieved liberty and prosperity.

When Fairfield told me the story, some years afterward, I asked him if he did not feel guilty of encouraging horse-stealing, as well as negro-stealing. I knew that death was the penalty for each of these crimes, according to the laws of Virginia and North Carolina.

The reply was: "No! I knew that Bill had earned several horses for his master, and he took only one. Bill had been a faithful fellow, and worked hard for many years, and that horse was all the pay he got. As to negro-stealing, I would steal all the slaves in Virginia if I could."

After spending several months in Ohio, John Fairfield returned to Virginia, but did not remain long. His uncle suspected him of having helped his able-bodied and valuable servant to escape, and having obtained evidence from some source—probably from Ohio—he set about procuring a writ and having his nephew arrested.

Fairfield learned of his uncle's intention, and concluded to leave that part of the country. Actuated by a feeling of spite, or some other motive, he resolved to take other slaves, as he had taken Bill, and succeeded in getting away with several, some of whom belonged to his uncle. They traveled during the night and hid themselves during the day. Sometimes when they were safely secreted for the day, Fairfield went forward a few miles and purchased provisions, under the pretense of buying for movers in camp; then returned and supplied the party of fugitives. They finally arrived safely in Canada, and Fairfield, liking the country, concluded to make his home there. Bill was now married and comfortably settled.

Fairfield's success in conducting the slaves from Virginia to Canada was soon known to many of the fugitives settled in that country, and having confidence in him, they importuned him to bring away from slavery the husbands, wives, children, or other relatives which they had left behind them in various parts of the South. Some of them had accumulated small sums of money, and offered to pay him if he would undertake the mission.

Fairfield was a young man without family, and was fond of adventure and excitement. He wanted employment, and agreed to take the money offered by the fugitives and engage in the undertaking. He obtained the names of masters and slaves, and an exact knowledge of the different localities to be visited, together with other information that might be of use to him; then acted as his shrewd judgment dictated, under different circumstances. He would go South, into the neighborhood where the slaves were whom he intended to conduct away, and, under an assumed name and a false pretense of business, engage boarding, perhaps at the house of the master whose stock of valuable property he intended to decrease. He would proclaim himself to be a Virginian, and profess to be strongly pro-slavery in his sentiments, thus lulling the suspicions of the slaveholders while he established a secret understanding with the slaves—gaining their confidence and making arrangements for their escape. Then he would suddenly disappear from the neighborhood, and several slaves would be missing at the same time.

Fairfield succeeded well in his daring adventures, and in many instances brought members of families together in Canada, who had been separated for several years. Husbands and wives were again united, and there were joyful meetings between parents and children. The fugitives settled in Canada had unbounded confidence in Fairfield, and were constantly begging him to bring away their friends and relatives from slavery. He continued this unique business for more than twelve years, and during that time aided, it is said, several thousand slaves to escape from bondage and reach Canada. He was a wicked man, daring and reckless in his actions, yet faithful to the trust reposed in him, and benevolent to the poor. He seemed to have no fear for his personal safety—was always ready to risk his life and liberty in order to rescue the slaves from bondage.

He was an inveterate hater of slavery, and this feeling supplied a motive for the actions of his whole life. He believed that every slave was justly entitled to freedom, and that if any person came between him and liberty, the slave had a perfect right to shoot him down. He always went heavily armed himself, and did not scruple to use his weapons whenever he thought the occasion required their use. He resorted to many stratagems to effect his object in the South, and brought away numbers of slaves from nearly every slave State in the Union. He often stopped at Cincinnati, on his way South, and generally made his home among the colored people. He frequently called to see me, and told me of his daring exploits and plans of operation, to all of which I objected. I could have no sympathy with his mode of action, and at various times urged him to cease his operations in the South and return to his home in Canada and remain there. I would have nothing to do with aiding him to carry out his plans, for I could not indorse the principles he acted upon.

At the time I did not believe half the stories that he told me; but afterward, learning from other sources of the many instances of his wonderful success, and knowing several of them from personal observation, and hearing stories from fugitives of their deliverance by his aid, I began to think that most of his stories might be true.

Fairfield was always ready to take money for his services from the slaves if they had it to offer, but if they did not he helped them all the same. Sometimes the slaves in the South had accumulated a little money, which they gave gladly to any one who would conduct them out of the house of bondage; and sometimes the fugitives in the North gave their little hoard to Fairfield, and begged him to rescue their relatives from slavery. Though always willing to take money for his services, he was equally ready to spend it in the same cause, and, if necessary, would part with his last dollar to effect his object. Fairfield had various methods of carrying out his plans. When he had obtained a list of the names of the slaves he wished to bring away, together with the names of their masters, and an exact knowledge of the different localities he was to visit in various parts of the South, he went to work without any hesitation, relying on his intimate knowledge of Southern customs to bear him safely through his perilous mission, and on his ingenuity and daring to extricate him from any difficulty he might fall into. Sometimes he engaged in some trading business and remained in the South six or twelve months at a time, familiarizing himself with different localities, making the acquaintance of the slaves and maturing his plans. At other times he would enter a neighborhood where he was an entire stranger, represent himself as a slave-dealer, and gain a knowledge of the slaves he wished to take away. He would make known his plans to them secretly, and some night they would leave their homes, and intrust themselves into his guidance. Fairfield would conduct them safely across the Ohio River, and after placing them on some branch of the Underground Railroad, and seeing them started toward Canada, he would return to the South, assume another name, and enter another neighborhood, to enact the same over again.

At one time he took a company of slaves from the northwestern part of Kentucky, and to elude pursuit made directly toward Nashville, Tennessee. The company consisted of able-bodied men, who were all well armed. They took horses belonging to their masters, and rode as far as they could the first night, then turned the horses loose and hid themselves during the day. The next night they took other horses, and so on, night after night, until they reached the Ohio River, near Maysville, Kentucky. Fairfield managed to get the men over the river and started safely on their way to Canada, then he returned to the South to continue his adventurous business.

At one time when he went South he had a few horses to sell, and took with him two able-bodied, free, colored men, whom he treated as his slaves, ordering them about in a peremptory manner. These men were shrewd and intelligent, and understood his plans. They ingratiated themselves with the slaves Fairfield had come to rescue, gained their confidence and ran off with them one dark night, steering their course to Canada by the north star. At other times Fairfield assumed to be returning from Louisiana, where he had been with a drove of slaves. He had with him, on such occasions, a body servant whom he professed to treat with great harshness, but who was really his confidant and accomplice. Through this servant he gained access to the slaves he wished to rescue.

Fairfield was several times betrayed and arrested, in the South, and put in prison, but being a Free Mason, high in the Order, he managed to get out of prison without being tried. He broke jail once or twice and escaped. He often had to endure privation and hardship, but was ready to undergo any suffering, for the sake of effecting his object. He sometimes divided his clothing with a destitute fugitive, and was willing to make any sacrifice of personal comfort. We often heard of his arrival in Canada with large companies of fugitives, whom he had conducted thither by some line of the Underground Railroad.

Fairfield was once betrayed and captured in Bracken County, Ken-

tucky, and put in prison, where he remained through a winter of unusual severity. Before the time for his trial came, he escaped from jail
by the aid of some of his friends, and crossed the Ohio River to Ripley. At the house of a noted abolitionist of that place, Fairfield lay sick
for two weeks, having taken a deep cold while confined in jail. When
he became well enough to travel he came to Cincinnati, and stopped
at the house of a colored friend. I went to see him and had a long talk
with him. I again advised him, to quit his hazardous work, in which
he constantly risked his life and liberty. I told him I had no sympathy
with his mode of operation, and urged him strongly to go home to
Canada, and never cross Mason and Dixon's line again. He did not
accept my advice, but swore that he would liberate a slave for every
day that he had lain in prison. Although a man of strong constitution
he appeared to be much broken in health by the hardships he had un-
dergone. After resting a few weeks and recruiting his strength, he disappeared from the city, and no one knew where he had gone.

The next news we had concerning him was that he had crossed the
Ohio River, near Lawrenceburg, with a party of twenty-eight fugitives, from Kentucky. . . . After that, we heard nothing more of Fairfield for some time. The following autumn I received a letter from
George D. Baptist, of Detroit, stating that Fairfield had just arrived
there with a company of thirty fugitives from the State of Missouri.

Free colored people in the Northern States who had relatives in
slavery heard of Fairfield's successful efforts, and applied to him to
bring their friends out of bondage, sometimes offering him several
hundred dollars. At one time I was told of one of Fairfield's adventures up the Kanawha River, near Charleston, Virginia. Several colored people in Ohio, who had relatives in slavery at and near the salt
works, importuned Fairfield to bring them away, and he at last yielded
to their frequent solicitations, and promised to make the attempt. He
knew that it would require some time to accomplish his object, as
there were several slaves to be rescued, and he laid his plans accordingly. He chose the early spring for the time of his action, as the water
was then flush in the Kanawha. Taking two free colored men with
him, whom he claimed as his slaves, he went to the salt works on the
Kanawha, and professing to be from Louisville, Kentucky, said that

he had come to engage in the salt trade. He contracted for the building of two boats and for salt with which to load them when finished. These arrangements afforded time for his colored men to become acquainted with the slaves he wished to rescue, gain their confidence, and mature the plans for their escape.

Some of the slaves were good boatmen, as also were Fairfield's men, and it was planned that when the first boat was finished, one of the slaves and one of Fairfield's men should get into it on Saturday night, and float down the river a short distance to a point agreed upon, and take in a company of slaves, both men and women. They were then to take advantage of the high water and swift current of the Kanawha, and make all possible speed to the Ohio River. This plan was carried out successfully. Search was made in the neighborhood on Sabbath for some of the missing slaves, but no clue was gained. The loss of the boat was not discovered till Monday morning.

When Fairfield learned that one of his boats and one of his men were gone, he affected to be much enraged, and accused his other man of having some knowledge of the affair, and threatened him with severe punishment. The man denied having any part in the plot, but Fairfield professed to doubt him, and said that he should watch him closely.

When the owners of the missing slaves learned that the boat was gone, they at once surmised that their servants had made their escape by that means, and as there was no steamboat going down the river that day, they sent horsemen in pursuit, hoping that the boat might be intercepted at the mouth of the river. But when the pursuers reached that point, they found the new boat tied on the opposite side of the river; the fugitives were gone, and no clue to their course could be obtained.

Fairfield remained at the salt works to await the completion of his other boat, and to watch his other negro servant, of whom he professed to be very distrustful. In a few days the boat was completed, and the next Saturday night it disappeared, together with Fairfield's negro man and ten or twelve slaves. Fairfield was now ruined! Both his boats and both his slaves were gone; and the loss of his property made him almost frantic. He started in hot pursuit, accompanied by several men, determined to capture the fugitives at any hazard. When they reached the Ohio River they found the boat tied to the bank on the Ohio side, but the fugitives were gone.

The pursuers ferried across the river, and, according to Fairfield's suggestion, divided company and took different routes, with the understanding that they were all to meet at a point designated. But Fairfield never met them, and was never seen at the salt works afterward. He well knew, however, where to meet the fugitives; all that had been previously arranged. After the search was over, he conducted them safely to Canada, *via* the Underground Railroad.

Soon afterward Fairfield performed another daring feat, east of the mountains. There were a number of fugitives in Canada, nearly white, who had come from Maryland, the District of Columbia and Virginia, and who had a number of relatives of the same complexion in the localities they had left. There were also some free people living in Detroit, who had mulatto and quadroon relatives in the localities mentioned. Fairfield had often been solicited by these fugitives and free people to bring their friends out of slavery, and he finally agreed to make the attempt if a sum of money was raised for him, sufficient to justify it. The amount was made up and paid to him, and he went East on his hazardous mission.

He spent some time making the acquaintance of these mulattoes and quadroons in the different neighborhoods, and maturing his plans for their escape. Most of them were bright and intelligent, and some of them had saved enough money to pay their passage to Canada. After gaining their confidence and making them acquainted with his plans, Fairfield went to Philadelphia and bought wigs and powder. These cost him eighty dollars—I afterward saw the bill. His first experiment with these articles of disguise was made at Baltimore. Having secretly collected the mulatto slaves of that city and vicinity, whom he had arranged to conduct to the North, he applied the powder and put on the wigs. The effect was satisfactory; the slaves looked like white people.

Fairfield bought tickets for them and they took the evening train to Harrisburg, where he had made arrangements for another person to meet them, who would accompany them to Cleveland and put them aboard the boat for Detroit.

Fairfield, having seen this party safely on the way, returned immediately to Washington City for another company, who, by the aid of wigs and powder, passed for white people. He put these fugitives on the train, and accompanied them to Pittsburg. I received a letter from a friend in Cleveland, informing me of the arrival of both these parties, through Fairfield's agency, which was the first intelligence I had of his operations in the East. From Pittsburg, Fairfield returned to Philadelphia, and finding that he had not enough money to complete his work, he applied to the abolition society of that city for assistance, but, as he was a stranger to them, they hesitated about granting his request.

He told them that Levi Coffin, of Cincinnati, knew him well. George W. Taylor telegraphed to me at once—"John Fairfield wants money; shall we give it to him?"

I replied: "If John Fairfield needs money, give it to him."

He was then furnished with the amount he called for, and made his way at once into Virginia, near Harper's Ferry, for the third company of slaves. One of this company was too dark to be transformed into a white person by means of a wig and powder, and Fairfield was compelled to leave him behind. He regretted to do so, but feared that his appearance would betray the others. Fairfield got the rest of the party to the railroad and took the express train for Pittsburg, but they were soon missed and the course they had taken was discovered. Their pursuers engaged an engine and one car, and followed the express train at full speed, hoping to overtake it and capture them before they reached Pittsburg. The engine overtook the train just as it was entering Pittsburg, but before the cars were fairly still, Fairfield and the fugitives sprang out and scattered, and ran in various directions through the city. The pursuers sprang out and gave chase, but did not succeed in capturing any of them. The fugitives soon found safe quarters among the abolitionists, and lay still for several days. Great efforts were made to find them, but they were unsuccessful, and the pursuers finally gave up the hunt and returned home. I received a letter from a friend in Pittsburg giving me these particulars, and shortly after learned that the fugitives had arrived in Cleveland. I also heard of their safe arrival in Detroit. A friend in that city wrote me that Fairfield had just reached there with the best looking company of fugitives that had ever passed through Detroit.

Thus, in numerous ways, John Fairfield was instrumental in rescuing hundreds of slaves from bondage, and in bringing together, in Canada, husbands and wives, parents and children, who had long been separated. He seemed to glory in the work, much as a military commander would in a victory over his enemies.

Although I could not sympathize with or encourage Fairfield's mode of operation, yet I often took in the fugitives whom he aided to escape. Some he brought himself; others traveled by his special directions, secreting themselves on steamboats or making the journey on foot. They generally reached our house in a state of destitution and distress, and we were always ready to succor them. In one instance John Fairfield came from a great distance, bringing a company of fugitives. They did encounter many dangers and hardships on the way, and had suffered much from hunger and exposure. Fairfield's money had all been expended, and his clothes were ragged and dirty; he looked like a fugitive himself. I took him and his company in, and after the fugitives rested and were fitted for the journey they were forwarded to Canada, *via* the Underground Railroad.

Fairfield remained in the city to recruit his strength and renew his clothing; he had left some money and clothing here when on his way South. The company referred to consisted of eight or ten brave, intelligent-looking slaves, who had determined to reach a land of liberty under the leadership of John Fairfield, or die in the attempt. Fairfield had spent some time in their neighborhood, buying eggs and chickens and shipping them to some point on the river. This was his ostensible business: his real errand was to get acquainted with the slaves. He had private interviews with them at night, in some secluded spot in the woods, and made all the plans and arrangements for the journey. Each one of the party he furnished with a revolver and plenty of ammunition.

One of the most intelligent of the fugitives said to me: "I never saw such a man as Fairfield. He told us he would take us out of slavery or die in the attempt, if we would do our part, which we promised to do. We all agreed to fight till we died, rather than be captured. Fairfield said he wanted no cowards in the company; if we were attacked and one of us showed cowardice or started to run, he would shoot him down."

They were attacked several times by patrolers, and fired upon, but always succeeded in driving the enemy and making their escape, keeping near their leader and obeying his commands. Fairfield said that they had a desperate battle one moonlight night with a company of armed men. They had been discovered by the patrolers, who had gathered a party of men and waylaid them at a bridge.

Fairfield said: "They were lying in ambush at each end of the bridge, and when we got fairly on the bridge they fired at us from each end. They thought, no doubt, that this sudden attack would intimidate us and that we would surrender, but in this they were mistaken. I ordered my men to charge to the front, and they did charge. We fired as we went, and the men in ambush scattered and ran like scared sheep."

"Was anybody hurt?" I asked.

In reply Fairfield showed me several bullet holes in his clothes, a slight flesh wound on one arm, and a slight flesh wound on the leg of one of the fugitives.

"You see," he said, "we were in close quarters, but my men were plucky. We shot to kill, and we made the devils run."

I reproved him for trying to kill any one. I told him it was better to suffer wrong than to do wrong, and that we should love our enemies.

"Love the devil!" he exclaimed. "Slaveholders are all devils, and it is no harm to kill the devil. I do not intend to hurt people if they keep out of the way, but if they step in between me and liberty, they must take the consequences. When I undertake to conduct slaves out of bondage I feel that it is my duty to defend them, even to the last drop of my blood."

I saw that it was useless to preach peace principles to John Fairfield. He would fight for the fugitives as long as his life lasted. When

Fairfield left Cincinnati I knew not where he went, and did not hear any news of him until some time the next year. I then learned that in the interval he had rescued slaves from Louisiana, Alabama, Mississippi and Georgia, who had been forwarded to Canada on the lines of the Underground Railroad leading through Illinois and Michigan, and that he had just arrived in Canada himself with a company of fugitives from the State of Missouri. Not long afterward Fairfield arrived in Cincinnati, bringing with him a party of slaves from Kentucky. He forwarded them on to Canada, and remained in the city to have the benefit of medical treatment. He had a hard cough, contracted, no doubt, by exposure and hardship, and his general health seemed shattered. I again urged him to quit the perilous business he had been engaged in, and he seemed inclined to accept my advice. He bought a few goods and opened a small store in Randolph County, Indiana, in the midst of a large settlement of free colored people, where he was well known.

He remained here for a year or two, then closed up his business and disappeared. It was thought in that neighborhood that he had gone to Canada, but we could never learn that he had been seen in Canada afterward. We supposed that when he left Indiana he went South. This was a short time before the Rebellion in 1861, and from that time to the present no news of Fairfield has been received by any of his friends. The conjecture is that he was killed in Tennessee, near the iron-works, on the Cumberland River. It was reported through the papers that there was an insurrectionary movement among the slaves in that locality; that a number of them had obtained arms; and an alarm started that the negroes were about to rise. This was sufficient to create great excitement in the whole neighborhood, and to bring out a little army of armed men to hunt the suspected negroes. Several negroes who attempted to defend themselves were shot; others were captured and hung by the infuriated mob. It was reported that a white man, supposed to be the instigator of the movement and the leader of the negroes, was found among them, and that he was killed. He was a stranger in that neighborhood, and his name was not known. I have always supposed that this man was John Fairfield, and that in this way his strange career was ended by a violent death. With all his faults and misguided impulses, and wicked ways, he was a brave man; he never betrayed a trust that was reposed in him, and he was a true friend to the oppressed and suffering slave.

VI.

Margaret Garner

◖ Perhaps no case that came under my notice, while engaged in aiding fugitive slaves, attracted more attention and aroused deeper interest and sympathy than the case of Margaret Garner, the slave mother, who killed her child rather than see it taken back to slavery. This happened in the latter part of January, 1856. The Ohio River was frozen over at the time, and the opportunity thus offered for escaping to a free State was embraced by a number of slaves living in Kentucky, several miles back from the river. A party of seventeen, belonging to different masters in the same neighborhood, made arrangements to escape together. There was snow on the ground and the roads were smooth, so the plan of going to the river on a sled naturally suggested itself. The time fixed for their flight was Sabbath night, and having managed to get a large sled and two good horses, belonging to one of their masters, the party of seventeen crowded into the sled and started on their hazardous journey in the latter part of the night. They drove the horses at full speed, and at daylight reached the river below Covington, opposite Western Row. They left the sled and horses here, and as quickly as possible crossed the river on foot. It was now broad daylight, and people were beginning to pass about the streets, and the fugitives divided their company that they might not attract so much notice.

An old slave man named Simon, and his wife Mary, together with their son Robert and his wife Margaret Garner and four children, made their way to the house of a colored man named Kite, who had formerly lived in their neighborhood and had been purchased from slavery by his father, Joe Kite. They had to make several inquiries in order to find Kite's house, which was below Mill Creek, in the lower part of the city. This afterward led to their discovery; they had been seen by a number of persons on their way to Kite's, and were easily traced by pursuers. The other nine fugitives were more fortunate. They made their way up town and found friends who conducted them to safe hiding-places, where they remained until night. They were then put on the Underground Railroad, and went safely through to Canada.

Kite felt alarmed for the safety of the party that had arrived at his house, and as soon as breakfast was over, he came to my store, at the corner of Sixth and Elm Streets, to ask counsel regarding them. I told him that they were in a very unsafe place and must be removed at once. I directed him how to conduct them from his house to the outskirts of the city, up Mill Creek, to a settlement of colored people in the western part of the city, where fugitives were often harbored. I would make arrangements to forward them northward, that night, on the Underground Railroad. Kite returned to his house at once, according to my directions, but he was too late; in a few minutes after his return, the house was surrounded by pursuers—the masters of the fugitives, with officers and a posse of men. The door and windows were barred, and those inside refused to give admittance. The fugitives were determined to fight, and to die, rather than to be taken back to slavery. Margaret, the mother of the four children, declared that she would kill herself and her children before she would return to bondage. The slave men were armed and fought bravely. The window was first battered down with a stick of wood, and one of the deputy marshals attempted to enter, but a pistol shot from within made a flesh wound on his arm and caused him to abandon the attempt. The pursuers then battered down the door with some timber and rushed in. The husband of Margaret fired several shots, and wounded one of the officers, but was soon overpowered and dragged out of the house. At this moment, Margaret Garner, seeing that their hopes of freedom were vain, seized a butcher knife that lay on the table, and with one stroke cut the throat of her little daughter, whom she probably loved the best. She then attempted to take the life of the other children and to kill herself, but she was overpowered and hampered before she could complete her desperate work. The whole party was then arrested and lodged in jail.

The trial lasted two weeks, drawing crowds to the court-room every day. Colonel Chambers, of this city, and two lawyers from Covington—Wall and Tinnell—appeared for the claimants, and Messrs. Jolliffe and Getchell for the slaves. The counsel for the defense brought witnesses to prove that the fugitives had been permitted to visit the city at various times previously. It was claimed that Margaret Garner had been brought here by her owners a number of years before, to act as nurse girl, and according to the law which liberated slaves who were brought into free States by the consent of their masters, she had been free from that time, and her children, all of whom had been born since then—following the condition of the mother—were likewise free.

The Commissioner decided that a voluntary return to slavery, after a visit to a free State, re-attached the conditions of slavery, and that the fugitives were legally slaves at the time of their escape.

Early in the course of the trial, Lawyer Jolliffe announced that warrants had been issued by the State authorities to arrest the fugitives on a criminal charge—Margaret Garner for murder, and the others for complicity in murder—and moved that the papers should be served on them immediately. Commissioner Pendery wished that to be deferred until he had given his decision, and the fugitives were out of the jurisdiction of his court, but Jolliffe pressed the motion to have the warrants served—"For," said he, "the fugitives have all assured me that they will *go singing to the gallows* rather than be returned to slavery." He further said that it might appear strange for him to be urging that his clients should be indicted for murder, but he was anxious that this charge should be brought against them before they passed from the jurisdiction of the Commissioner's Court, for the infamous law of 1850 provided that no warrant in any event should be served upon the fugitives in case they were remanded to the custody of their owners. Not even a warrant for murder could prevent their being returned to bondage.

Jolliffe said that in the final argument of the case he intended not only to allege, but to demonstrate, conclusively, to the Court, that the Fugitive Slave law was unconstitutional, and as part and parcel of that argument he wished to show the effects of carrying it out. It had driven a frantic mother to murder her own child rather than see it carried back to the seething hell of American slavery. This law was of such an order that its execution required human hearts to be wrung and human blood to be spilt.

"The Constitution," said he, "expressly declared that Congress should pass no law prescribing any form of religion or preventing the free exercise thereof. If Congress could not pass any law requiring you to worship God, still less could they pass one requiring you to carry fuel to hell." These ringing words called forth applause from all parts of the court-room. Jolliffe said: "It is for the Court to decide whether the Fugitive Slave law overrides the law of Ohio to such an extent that it can not arrest a fugitive slave even for a crime of murder."

The fugitives were finally indicted for murder, but we will see that this amounted to nothing.

Margaret Garner, the chief actor in the tragedy which had occurred, naturally excited much attention. She was a mulatto, about five feet high, showing one-fourth or one-third white blood. She had a high forehead, her eyebrows were finely arched and her eyes bright and intelligent, but the African appeared in the lower part of her face, in her broad nose and thick lips. On the left side of her forehead was an old scar, and on the cheek-bone, on the same side, another one. When asked what caused them, she said: "White man struck me." That was all, but it betrays a story of cruelty and degradation, and, perhaps, gives the key-note to Margaret's hate of slavery, her revolt against its thralldom, and her resolve to die rather than go back to it.

She appeared to be twenty-two or twenty-three years old. While in the court-room she was dressed in dark calico, with a white handkerchief pinned around her neck, and a yellow cotton handkerchief arranged as a turban, around her head. The babe she held in her arms was a little girl, about nine months old, and was much lighter in color than herself, light enough to show a red tinge in its cheeks. During the trial she would look up occasionally, for an instant, with a timid, apprehensive glance at the strange faces around her, but her eyes were generally cast down. The babe was continually fondling her face with its little hands, but she rarely noticed it, and her general expression was one of extreme sadness. The little boys, four and six years old, respectively, were bright-eyed, woolly-headed little fellows, with fat dimpled cheeks. During the trial they sat on the floor near their mother, playing together in happy innocence, all unconscious of the gloom that shrouded their mother, and of the fact that their own future liberty was at stake. The murdered child was almost white, a little girl of rare beauty.

The case seemed to stir every heart that was alive to the emotions of humanity. The interest manifested by all classes was not so much for the legal principles involved, as for the mute instincts that mold every human heart—the undying love of freedom that is planted in every breast—the resolve to die rather than submit to a life of degradation and bondage.

A number of people, who were deeply interested in the fugitives, visited them in prison and conversed with them. Old Simon, his wife Mary, and their son Robert, while expressing their longing for freedom, said that they should not attempt to kill themselves if they were returned to slavery. Their trust in God seemed to have survived all the wrong and cruelty inflicted upon them by man, and though they felt often like crying bitterly, "How long, O Lord, how long?" they still trusted and endured. But Margaret seemed to have a different nature; she could see nothing but woe for herself and her children. Who can fathom the depths of her heart as she brooded over the wrongs and insults that had been heaped upon her all her life? Who can wonder if her faith staggered when she saw her efforts to gain freedom frustrated, when she saw the gloom of her old life close around her again, without any hope of deliverance? Those who came to speak words of comfort and cheer felt them die upon their lips, when they looked into her face, and marked its expression of settled despair. Her sorrow was beyond the reach of any words of encouragement and consolation, and can be realized in all its fullness only by those who have tasted of a cup equally bitter.

Among those who visited Margaret in prison was Lucy Stone, the well-known eloquent public speaker. It was reported that she gave

Margaret a knife, and told her to kill herself and her children rather than be taken back to slavery. Colonel Chambers, the counsel for the claimants, referred to this rumor in court, and Lucy Stone, coming in shortly afterward, was informed of it. She requested to say a few words in reply, and when the court had adjourned, the greater part of the crowd remained to hear her. She said: "I am only sorry that I was not in when Colonel Chambers said what he did about me, and my giving a knife to Margaret. When I saw that poor fugitive, took her toil-hardened hand in mine, and read in her face deep suffering and an ardent longing for freedom, I could not help bid her be of good cheer. I told her that a thousand hearts were aching for her, and that they were glad one child of hers was safe with the angels. Her only reply was a look of deep despair, of anguish such as no words can speak. I thought the spirit she manifested was the same with that of our ancestors to whom we had erected the monument at Bunker Hill—the spirit that would rather let us all go back to God than back to slavery. The faded faces of the negro children tell too plainly to what degradation female slaves must submit. Rather than give her little daughter to that life, she killed it. If in her deep maternal love she felt the impulse to send her child back to God, to save it from coming woe, who shall say she had no right to do so? That desire had its root in the deepest and holiest feelings of our nature—implanted alike in black and white by our common Father. With my own teeth I would tear open my veins and let the earth drink my blood, rather than to wear the chains of slavery. How then could I blame her for wishing her child to find freedom with God and the angels, where no chains are? I know not whether this Commissioner has children, else I would appeal to him to know how he would feel to have them torn from him, but I feel that he will not disregard the Book which says: 'Thou shalt not deliver unto his master the servant which is escaped from his master unto thee: he shall dwell with thee, even among you, in that place which he shall choose in one of thy gates, where it liketh him best.'"

But in spite of touching appeals, of eloquent pleadings, the Commissioner remanded the fugitives back to slavery. He said that it was not a question of feeling to be decided by the chance current of his sympathies; the law of Kentucky and of the United States made it a question of property.

In regard to the claim, plainly established by the evidence, that the fugitives had previously been brought to this State by the consent of their masters, he said: "Had the slaves asserted their freedom, they would have been practically free, but they voluntarily returned to slavery. In allowing them to come to Ohio, the master voluntarily abandoned his claim upon them, and they, in returning, abandoned their claim to freedom."

By a provision of the law, previously referred to, they could not be tried on the warrant for murder, and their indictment on that charge was practically ignored. Jolliffe said, indignantly, that even a savage tribe reserved to itself the right to investigate a charge for murder committed within its border, but the sovereign State of Ohio allowed itself and its laws to be overruled by the infamous Fugitive Slave law, made in the interests of slaveholders. The question of bringing the case before a superior court, and trying the slaves for murder was agitated, and Gaines, the master of Margaret, promised to have her in safe-keeping on the opposite side of the river, to be delivered up to the authorities of the State of Ohio, if a requisition for her was made.

The fugitives were then delivered to their owners, who conveyed them in an omnibus to the wharf of the Covington ferry-boat. A crowd followed them to the river, but there was no demonstration. The masters were surrounded by large numbers of their Kentucky friends, who had stood by them and guarded their interests during the trial, and there was great rejoicing among them, on account of their victory.

The masters kept their slaves in jail in Covington, a few days, then took them away. When the requisition was made for Margaret, Gaines said that he had kept her in Covington for some time according to the agreement, then, as the writ was not served, he had sent her down the river. This was a violation of the spirit of the agreement, and much indignation was manifested by Margaret's friends in Ohio, but nothing further was done. Margaret was lost, in what Jolliffe called, "the seething hell of American slavery." It was reported that on her way down the river she sprang from the boat into the water with her babe in her arms; that when she rose she was seized by some of the boat hands and rescued, but that her child was drowned.

After the trial of the fugitives, a committee of citizens presented a purse to Jolliffe, accompanied by an address, in token of their appreciation of his services. He returned thanks in an eloquent letter, setting forth his views on the unconstitutionality of the Fugitive Slave law.

The

Underground Rail Road

A RECORD

OF

FACTS, AUTHENTIC NARRATIVES, LETTERS, &C.,

NARRATING THE HARDSHIPS HAIR-BREADTH ESCAPES

AND DEATH STRUGGLES

OF THE

SLAVES IN THEIR EFFORTS FOR FREEDOM

BY

WILLIAM STILL

Clarissa Davis

ARRIVED DRESSED IN MALE ATTIRE

Clarissa fled from Portsmouth, Va., in May, 1854, with two of her brothers. Two months and a half before she succeeded in getting off, Clarissa had made a desperate effort, but failed. The brothers succeeded, but she was left. She had not given up all hope of escape, however, and therefore sought "a safe hiding-place until an opportunity might offer," by which she could follow her brothers on the U. G. R. R. Clarissa was owned by Mrs. Brown and Mrs. Burkley, of Portsmouth, under whom she had always served.

Of them she spoke favorably, saying that she "had not been used as hard as many others were." At this period, Clarissa was about twenty-two years of age, of a bright brown complexion, with handsome features, exceedingly respectful and modest, and possessed all the characteristics of a well-bred young lady. For one so little acquainted with books as she was, the correctness of her speech was perfectly astonishing.

For Clarissa and her two brothers a "reward of one thousand dollars" was kept standing in the papers for a length of time, as these (articles) were considered very rare and valuable; the best that could be produced in Virginia.

In the meanwhile the brothers had passed safely on to New Bedford, but Clarissa remained secluded, "waiting for the storm to subside." Keeping up courage day by day, for seventy-five days, with the fear of being detected and severely punished, and then sold, after all her hopes and struggles, required the faith of a martyr. Time after time, when she hoped to succeed in making her escape, ill luck seemed to disappoint her, and nothing but intense suffering appeared

to be in store. Like many others, under the crushing weight of oppression, she thought she "should have to die" ere she tasted liberty.
In this state of mind, one day, word was conveyed to her that the
steamship, City of Richmond, had arrived from Philadelphia, and
that the steward on board (with whom she was acquainted), had consented to secrete her this trip, if she could manage to reach the ship
safely, which was to start the next day. This news to Clarissa was both
cheering and painful. She had been "praying all the time while waiting," but now she felt "that if it would only rain right hard the next
morning about three o'clock, to drive the police officers off the street,
then she could safely make her way to the boat." Therefore she prayed
anxiously all that day that it would rain, "but no sign of rain appeared
till towards midnight." The prospect looked horribly discouraging;
but she prayed on, and at the appointed hour (three o'clock—before
day), the rain descended in torrents. Dressed in male attire, Clarissa
left the miserable coop where she had been almost without light or air
for two and a half months, and unmolested, reached the boat safely,
and was secreted in a box by Wm. Bagnal, a clever young man who
sincerely sympathized with the slave, having a wife in slavery himself;
and by him she was safely delivered into the hands of the Vigilance
Committee.

Clarissa Davis here, by advice of the Committee, dropped her old
name, and was straightway christened "Mary D. Armstead." Desir-
ing to join her brothers and sister in New Bedford, she was duly furnished with her U. G. R. R. passport and directed thitherward. Her
father, who was left behind when she got off, soon after made his way
on North, and joined his children. He was too old and infirm probably to be worth anything, and had been allowed to go free, or to purchase himself for a mere nominal sum. Slaveholders would, on some
such occasions, show wonderful liberality in letting their old slaves go
free, when they could work no more. After reaching New Bedford,
Clarissa manifested her gratitude in writing to her friends in Philadelphia repeatedly, and evinced a very lively interest in the U. G. R. R.
The appended letter indicates her sincere feelings of gratitude and
deep interest in the cause—

William Still

NEW BEDFORD, August 26, 1855.

MR. STILL:—I avail my self to write you thes few lines hopeing they may find you and your family well as they leaves me very well and all the family well except my father he seams to be improveing with his shoulder he has been able to work a little I received the papers I was highly delighted to receive them I was very glad to hear from you in the wheler case I was very glad to hear that the persons ware safe I was very sory to hear that mr Williamson was put in prison but I know if the praying part of the people will pray for him and if he will put his trust in the lord he will bring him out more than conquer please remember my Dear old farther and sisters and brother to your family kiss the children for me I hear that the yellow fever is very bad down south now if the underground railroad could have free course the emergrant would cross the river of gordan rapidly I hope it may continue to run and I hope the wheels of the car may be greesed with more substantial greese so they may run over swiftly I would have wrote before but circumstances would not permit me Miss Sanders and all the friends desired to be remembered to you and your family I shall be pleased to hear from the underground rail road often

Yours respectfully,   MARY D. ARMSTEAD.

Anthony Blow, Alias
Henry Levison

SECRETED TEN MONTHS BEFORE STARTING—EIGHT DAYS
STOWED AWAY ON A STEAMER BOUND FOR PHILADELPHIA

⊂⊒ Arrived from Norfolk, about the 1st of November, 1854. Ten
months before starting, Anthony had been closely concealed. He belonged to the estate of Mrs. Peters, a widow, who had been dead
about one year before his concealment.

On the settlement of his old mistress' estate, which was to take
place one year after her death, Anthony was to be transferred to Mrs.
Lewis, a daughter of Mrs. Peters (the wife of James Lewis, Esq.).
Anthony felt well satisfied that he was not the slave to please the
"tyrannical whims" of his anticipated master, young Lewis, and of
course he hated the idea of having to come under his yoke. And what
made it still more unpleasant for Anthony was that Mr. Lewis would
frequently remind him that it was his intention to "sell him as soon as
he got possession—the first day of January." "I can get fifteen hundred dollars for you easily, and I will do it." This contemptuous threat
had caused Anthony's blood to boil time and again. But Anthony had
to take the matter as calmly as possible, which, however, he was not always able to do.

At any rate, Anthony concluded that his "young master had
counted the chickens before they were hatched." Indeed here Anthony began to be a deep thinker. He thought, for instance, that he
had already been shot three times, at the instance of slave-holders.
The first time he was shot was for refusing a flogging when only
eighteen years of age. The second time, he was shot in the head with
squirrel shot by the sheriff, who was attempting to arrest him for hav-

ing resisted three "young white ruffians," who wished to have the pleasure of beating him, but got beaten themselves. And in addition to being shot this time, Anthony was still further "broke in" by a terrible flogging from the Sheriff. The third time Anthony was shot he was about twenty-one years of age. In this instance he was punished for his old offence—he "would not be whipped."

This time his injury from being shot was light, compared with the two preceding attacks. Also in connection with these murderous conflicts, he could not forget that he had been sold on the auction block. But he had still deeper thinking to do yet. He determined that his young master should never get "fifteen hundred dollars for him on the 1st of January," unless he got them while he (Anthony) was running. For Anthony had fully made up his mind that when the last day of December ended, his bondage should end also, even if he should have to accept death as a substitute. He then began to think of the Underground Rail Road and of Canada; but who the agents were, or how to find the depot, was a serious puzzle to him. But his time was getting so short he was convinced that whatever he did would have to be done quickly. In this frame of mind he found a man who professed to know something about the Underground Rail Road, and for "thirty dollars" promised to aid him in the matter.

The thirty dollars were raised by the hardest effort and passed over to the pretended friend, with the expectation that it would avail greatly in the emergency. But Anthony found himself sold for thirty dollars, as nothing was done for him. However, the 1st day of January arrived, but Anthony was not to be found to answer to his name at roll call. He had "took out" very early in the morning. Daily he prayed in his place of concealment how to find the U. G. R. R. Ten months passed away, during which time he suffered almost death, but persuaded himself to believe that even that was better than slavery. With Anthony, as it had been with thousands of others similarly situated, just as everything was looking the most hopeless, word came to him in his place of concealment that a friend named Minkins, employed on the steamship City of Richmond, would undertake to conceal him on the boat, if he could be crowded in a certain place, which was about the only spot that would be perfectly safe. This was glorious news to

Anthony; but it was well for him that he was ignorant of the situation that awaited him on the boat, or his heart might have failed him. He was willing, however, to risk his life for freedom, and, therefore, went joyfully.

The hiding-place was small and he was large. A sitting attitude was the only way he could possibly occupy it. He was contented. This place was "near the range, directly over the boiler," and of course, was very warm. Nevertheless, Anthony felt that he would not murmur, as he knew what suffering was pretty well, and especially as he took it for granted that he would be free in about a day and a half—the usual time it took the steamer to make her trip. At the appointed hour the steamer left Norfolk for Philadelphia, with Anthony sitting flat down in his U. G. R. R. berth, thoughtful and hopeful. But before the steamer had made half her distance the storm was tossing the ship hither and thither fearfully. Head winds blew terribly, and for a number of days the elements seemed perfectly mad. In addition to the extraordinary state of the weather, when the storm subsided the fog took its place and held the mastery of the ship with equal despotism until the end of over seven days, when finally the storm, wind, and fog all disappeared, and on the eighth day of her boisterous passage the steamship City of Richmond landed at the wharf of Philadelphia, with this giant and hero on board who had suffered for ten months in his concealment on land and for eight days on the ship.

Anthony was of very powerful physical proportions, being six feet three inches in height, quite black, very intelligent, and of a temperament that would not submit to slavery. For some years his master, Col. Cunnagan, had hired him out in Washington, where he was accused of being in the schooner Pearl, with Capt. Drayton's memorable "seventy fugitives on board, bound for Canada." At this time he was stoker in a machine shop, and was at work on an anchor weighing "ten thousand pounds." In the excitement over the attempt to escape in the Pearl, many were arrested, and the officers with irons visited Anthony at the machine shop to arrest him, but he declined to let them put the hand-cuffs on him, but consented to go with them, if permitted to do so without being ironed. The officers yielded, and Anthony went willingly to the jail. Passing unnoticed other interesting conflicts in his hard life, suffice it to say, he left his wife, Ann, and three children, Benjamin, John and Alfred, all owned by Col. Cunnagan. In this bravehearted man, the Committee felt a deep interest, and accorded him their usual hospitalities.

Henry Box Brown

☞ Although the name of Henry Box Brown has been echoed over the land for a number of years, and the simple facts connected with his marvelous escape from slavery in a box published widely through the medium of anti-slavery papers, nevertheless it is not unreasonable to suppose that very little is generally known in relation to this case.

Briefly, the facts are these, which doubtless have never before been fully published—

Brown was a man of invention as well as a hero. In point of interest, however, his case is no more remarkable than many others. Indeed, neither before nor after escaping did he suffer one-half what many others have experienced.

He was decidedly an unhappy piece of property in the city of Richmond, Va. In the condition of a slave he felt that it would be impossible for him to remain. Full well did he know, however, that it was no holiday task to escape the vigilance of Virginia slave-hunters, or the wrath of an enraged master for committing the unpardonable sin of attempting to escape to a land of liberty. So Brown counted well the cost before venturing upon this hazardous undertaking. Ordinary modes of travel he concluded might prove disastrous to his hopes; he, therefore, hit upon a new invention altogether, which was to have himself boxed up and forwarded to Philadelphia direct by express. The size of the box and how it was to be made to fit him most comfortably, was of his own ordering. Two feet eight inches deep, two feet wide, and three feet long were the exact dimensions of the box, lined with baize. His resources with regard to food and water consisted of the following: One bladder of water and a few small biscuits.

His mechanical implement to meet the death-struggle for fresh air, all told, was one large gimlet. Satisfied that it would be far better to peril his life for freedom in this way than to remain under the galling yoke of Slavery, he entered his box, which was safely nailed up and hooped with five hickory hoops, and was then addressed by his next friend, James A. Smith, a shoe dealer, to Wm. H. Johnson, Arch street, Philadelphia, marked, "This side up with care." In this condition he was sent to Adams' Express office in a dray, and thence by overland express to Philadelphia. It was twenty-six hours from the time he left Richmond until his arrival in the City of Brotherly Love. The notice, "This side up, &c.," did not avail with the different expressmen, who hesitated not to handle the box in the usual rough manner common to this class of men. For a while they actually had the box upside down, and had him on his head for miles. A few days before he was expected, certain intimation was conveyed to a member of the Vigilance Committee that a box might be expected by the three o'clock morning train from the South, which might contain a man. One of the most serious walks he ever took—and they had not been a few—to meet and accompany passengers, he took at half past two o'clock that morning to the depot. Not once, but for more than a score of times, he fancied the slave would be dead. He anxiously looked while the freight was being unloaded from the cars, to see if he could recognize a box that might contain a man; one alone had that appearance, and he confessed it really seemed as if there was the scent of death about it. But on inquiry, he soon learned that it was not the one he was looking after, and he was free to say he experienced a marked sense of relief. That same afternoon, however, he received from Richmond a telegram, which read thus, "Your case of goods is shipped and will arrive to-morrow morning."

At this exciting juncture of affairs, Mr. McKim, who had been engineering this important undertaking, deemed it expedient to change the programme slightly in one particular at least to insure greater safety. Instead of having a member of the Committee go again to the depot for the box, which might excite suspicion, it was decided that it

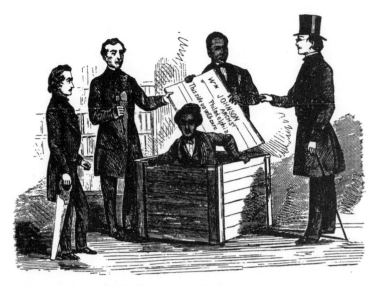

RESURRECTION OF HENRY BOX BROWN
[William Still is shown holding the lid of the box.]

would be safest to have the express bring it direct to the Anti-Slavery Office.

But all apprehension of danger did not now disappear, for there was no room to suppose that Adams' Express office had any sympathy with the Abolitionist or the fugitive, consequently for Mr. McKim to appear personally at the express office to give directions with reference to the coming of a box from Richmond which would be directed to Arch street, and yet not intended for that street, but for the Anti-Slavery office at 107 North Fifth street, it needed of course no great discernment to foresee that a step of this kind was wholly impracticable and that a more indirect and covert method would have to be adopted. In this dreadful crisis Mr. McKim, with his usual good judgment and remarkably quick, strategical mind, especially in matters pertaining to the U. G. R. R., hit upon the following plan, namely, to go to his friend, E. M. Davis,* who was then extensively

---

*E. M. Davis was a member of the Executive Committee of the Pennsylvania Anti-Slavery Society and a long-tried Abolitionist, son-in-law of James and Lucretia Mott.

engaged in mercantile business, and relate the circumstances. Having daily intercourse with said Adams' Express office, and being well acquainted with the firm and some of the drivers, Mr. Davis could, as Mr. McKim thought, talk about "boxes, freight, etc.," from any part of the country without risk. Mr. Davis heard Mr. McKim's plan and instantly approved of it, and was heartily at his service.

"Dan, an Irishman, one of Adams' Express drivers, is just the fellow to go to the depot after the box," said Davis. "He drinks a little too much whiskey sometimes, but he will do anything I ask him to do, promptly and obligingly. I'll trust Dan, for I believe he is the very man." The difficulty which Mr. McKim had been so anxious to overcome was thus pretty well settled. It was agreed that Dan should go after the box next morning before daylight and bring it to the Anti-Slavery office direct, and to make it all the more agreeable for Dan to get up out of his warm bed and go on this errand before day, it was decided that he should have a five dollar gold piece for himself. Thus these preliminaries having been satisfactorily arranged, it only remained for Mr. Davis to see Dan and give him instructions accordingly, etc.

Next morning, according to arrangement, the box was at the Anti-Slavery office in due time. The witnesses present to behold the resurrection were J. M. McKim, Professor C. D. Cleveland, Lewis Thompson, and the writer.

Mr. McKim was deeply interested; but having been long identified with the Anti-Slavery cause as one of its oldest and ablest advocates in the darkest days of slavery and mobs, and always found by the side of the fugitive to counsel and succor, he was on this occasion perfectly composed.

Professor Cleveland, however, was greatly moved. His zeal and earnestness in the cause of freedom, especially in rendering aid to passengers, knew no limit. Ordinarily he could not too often visit these travelers, shake them too warmly by the hand, or impart to them too freely of his substance to aid them on their journey. But now his emotion was overpowering.

Mr. Thompson, of the firm of Merrihew & Thompson—about the only printers in the city who for many years dared to print such incendiary documents as anti-slavery papers and pamphlets—one of the truest friends of the slave, was composed and prepared to witness the scene.

All was quiet. The door had been safely locked. The proceedings commenced. Mr. McKim rapped quietly on the lid of the box and called out, "All right!" Instantly came the answer from within, "All right, sir!"

The witnesses will never forget that moment. Saw and hatchet quickly had the five hickory hoops cut and the lid off, and the marvellous resurrection of Brown ensued. Rising up in his box, he reached out his hand, saying, "How do you do, gentlemen?" The little assemblage hardly knew what to think or do at that moment. He was about as wet as if he had come up out of the Delaware. Very soon he remarked that, before leaving Richmond he had selected for his arrival-hymn (if he lived) the Psalm beginning with these words: *"I waited patiently for the Lord, and He heard my prayer."* And most touchingly did he sing the psalm, much to his own relief, as well as to the delight of his small audience.

He was then christened Henry Box Brown, and soon afterwards was sent to the hospitable residence of James Mott and E. M. Davis, on Ninth street, where, it is needless to say, he met a most cordial reception from Mrs. Lucretia Mott and her household. Clothing and creature comforts were furnished in abundance, and delight and joy filled all hearts in that stronghold of philanthropy.

As he had been so long doubled up in the box he needed to promenade considerably in the fresh air, so James Mott put one of his broad-brim hats on his head and tendered him the hospitalities of his yard as well as his house, and while Brown promenaded the yard flushed with victory, great was the joy of his friends.

After his visit at Mr. Mott's, he spent two days with the writer, and then took his departure for Boston, evidently feeling quite conscious of the wonderful feat he had performed, and at the same time it may be safely said that those who witnessed this strange resurrection were not only elated at his success, but were made to sympathize more deeply than ever before with the slave. Also the noble-hearted Smith who boxed him up was made to rejoice over Brown's victory, and was thereby encouraged to render similar service to two other young bondmen, who appealed to him for deliverance. But, unfortunately, in this attempt the undertaking proved a failure. Two boxes containing the young men alluded to above, after having been duly expressed and some distance on the road, were, through the agency of the telegraph, betrayed, and the heroic young fugitives were captured in their boxes and dragged back to hopeless bondage. Consequently, through this deplorable failure, Samuel A. Smith was arrested, imprisoned, and was called upon to suffer severely, as may be seen from the subjoined correspondence, taken from the New York Tribune soon after his release from the penitentiary.

THE DELIVERER OF BOX BROWN—MEETING OF THE
COLORED CITIZENS OF PHILADELPHIA
[CORRESPONDENCE OF THE N. Y. TRIBUNE]

PHILADELPHIA, Saturday, July 5, 1856.
Samuel A. Smith, who boxed up Henry Box Brown in Richmond, Va., and forwarded him by overland express to Philadelphia, and who was arrested and convicted, eight years ago, for boxing up two other slaves, also directed to Philadelphia, having served out his imprisonment in the Penitentiary, was released on the 18th ultimo, and arrived in this city on the 21st.

Though he lost all his property; though he was refused witnesses on his trial (no officer could be found, who would serve a summons on a witness); though for five long months, in hot weather, he was kept heavily chained in a cell four by eight feet in dimensions; though he received five dreadful stabs, aimed at his heart, by a bribed assassin, nevertheless he still rejoices in the motives which prompted him to "undo the heavy burdens, and let the oppressed go free." Having resided nearly all his life in the South, where he had traveled and seen much of the "peculiar institution," and had witnessed the most horrid enormities inflicted upon the slave, whose cries were ever ringing in his ears, and for whom he had the warmest sympathy, Mr. Smith could not refrain from believing that the black man, as well as the white, had God-given rights. Consequently, he was not accustomed to shed tears when a poor creature escaped from his "kind master;" nor was he willing to turn a deaf ear to his appeals and groans, when he knew he was thirsting for freedom. From 1828 up to the day he was incarcerated, many had sought his aid and counsel, nor had they sought in vain. In various places he operated with success. In Richmond, however, it seemed expedient to invent a new plan for certain emergencies, hence the Box and Express plan was devised, at the instance of a few heroic slaves, who had manifested their willingness to die in a box, on the road to liberty, rather than continue longer under the yoke. But these heroes fell into the power of their enemies. Mr. Smith had not been long in the Penitentiary before he had fully gained the esteem and confidence of the Superintendent and other officers. Finding him to be humane and generous-hearted—showing kindness toward all, especially in buying bread, &c., for the starving prisoners, and by a timely note of warning, which had saved the life of one of the keepers, for whose destruction a bold plot had been arranged—the officers felt disposed to show him such favors as the law would allow. But their good intentions were soon frustrated. The Inquisition (commonly called the Legislature), being in session in Richmond, hearing that the Superintendent had been speaking well of Smith, and circulating a petition for his pardon, indignantly demanded to know if the rumor was well founded. Two weeks were spent by the Inquisition, and many witnesses were placed upon oath, to solemnly testify in the matter. One of the keepers swore that his life had been saved by Smith. Col. Morgan, the Superintendent, frequently testified in writing and verbally to Smith's good deportment; acknowledging that he had circulated petitions, &c.; and took the position, that he sincerely believed, that it would be to the interest of the institution to pardon him; calling the attention of the Inquisition, at the same time, to the fact, that not unfrequently pardons had been granted to criminals, under sentence of death, for the most cold-blooded murder, to say nothing of other gross crimes. The effort for pardon was soon abandoned, for the following reason given by the Governor: "I can't, and I won't pardon him!"

In view of the unparalleled injustice which Mr. S. had suffered, as well as on account of the aid he had rendered to the slaves, on his arrival in this city the colored citizens of Philadelphia felt that he was entitled to sympathy and aid, and straightway invited him to remain a few days, until arrangements could be made for a mass meeting to receive him. Accordingly, on last Monday evening, a mass meeting convened in the Israel church, and the Rev. Wm. T. Catto was called to the chair, and Wm. Still was appointed secretary. The chairman briefly stated the object of the meeting. Having lived in the South, he claimed to know something of the workings of the oppressive system of slavery generally, and declared that, notwithstanding the many exposures of the evil which came under his own observation, the most vivid descriptions fell far short of the realities his own eyes had witnessed. He then introduced Mr. Smith, who arose and in a plain manner briefly told his story, assuring the audience that he had always hated slavery, and had taken great pleasure in helping many out of it, and though he had suffered much physically and peculiarly for the cause' sake, yet he murmured not, but rejoiced in what he had done. After taking his seat, addresses were made by the Rev. S. Smith, Messrs. Kinnard, Brunner, Bradway, and others. The following preamble and resolutions were adopted—

> WHEREAS, We, the colored citizens of Philadelphia, have among us Samuel A. Smith, who was incarcerated over seven years in the Richmond Penitentiary, for doing an act that was honorable to his feelings and his sense of justice and humanity, therefore,
>
> *Resolved,* That we welcome him to this city as a martyr to the cause of Freedom.
>
> *Resolved,* That we heartily tender him our gratitude for the good he has done to our suffering race.
>
> *Resolved,* That we sympathize with him in his losses and sufferings in the cause of the poor, down-trodden slave.
>
> W. S.

During his stay in Philadelphia, on this occasion, he stopped for about a fortnight with the writer, and it was most gratifying to learn from him that he was no new worker on the U. G. R. R. But that he had long hated slavery thoroughly, and although surrounded with perils on every side, he had not failed to help a poor slave whenever the opportunity was presented.

Pecuniary aid, to some extent, was rendered him in this city, for which he was grateful, and after being united in marriage, by Wm. H. Furness, D.D., to a lady who had remained faithful to him through all his sore trials and sufferings, he took his departure for Western New York, with a good conscience and an unshaken faith in the belief that in aiding his fellow-man to freedom he had but simply obeyed the word of Him who taught man to do unto others as he would be done by.

The Arrivals of a Single Month

SIXTY PASSENGERS CAME IN ONE MONTH—TWENTY-
EIGHT IN ONE ARRIVAL—GREAT PANIC AND INDIGNATION
MEETING—INTERESTING CORRESPONDENCE FROM
MASTERS AND FUGITIVES

☞ The great number of cases to be here noticed forbids more than a brief reference to each passenger. As they arrived in parties, their narratives will be given in due order as found on the book of records:

William Griffen, Henry Moor, James Camper, Noah Ennells and Levin Parker. This party came from Cambridge, Md.

WILLIAM is thirty-four years of age, of medium size and substantial appearance. He fled from James Waters, Esq., a lawyer, living in Cambridge. He was "wealthy, close, and stingy," and owned nine head of slaves and a farm, on which William served. He was used very hard, which was the cause of his escape, though the idea that he was entitled to his freedom had been entertained for the previous twelve years. On preparing to take the Underground, he armed himself with a big butcher-knife, and resolved, if attacked, to make his enemies stand back. His master was a member of the Methodist Church.

HENRY is tall, copper-colored, and about thirty years of age. He complained not so much of bad usage as of the utter distaste he had to working all the time for the "white people for nothing." He was also decidedly of the opinion that every man should have his liberty. Four years ago his wife was "sold away to Georgia" by her young master; since which time not a word had he heard of her. She left three children, and he, in escaping, also had to leave them in the same hands that sold their mother. He was owned by Levin Dale, a farmer near

Cambridge. Henry was armed with a six-barreled revolver, a large knife, and a determined mind.

JAMES is twenty-four years of age, quite black, small size, keen look, and full of hope for the "best part of Canada." He fled from Henry Hooper, "a dashing young man and a member of the Episcopal Church." Left because he "did not enjoy privileges" as he wished to do. He was armed with two pistols and a dirk to defend himself.

NOAH is only nineteen, quite dark, well-proportioned, and possessed of a fair average of common sense. He was owned by "Blackhead Bill LeCount," who "followed drinking, chewing tobacco, catching 'runaways,' and hanging around the court-house." However, he owned six head of slaves, and had a "rough wife," who belonged to the Methodist Church. Left because he "expected every day to be sold"—his master being largely in "debt." Brought with him a butcher-knife.

LEVIN is twenty-two, rather short built, medium size and well colored. He fled from Lawrence G. Colson, "a very bad man, fond of drinking, great to fight and swear, and hard to please." His mistress was "real rough; very bad, worse than he was as 'fur' as she could be." Having been stinted with food and clothing and worked hard, was the apology offered by Levin for running off.

STEBNEY SWAN, John Stinger, Robert Emerson, Anthony Pugh and Isabella ———. This company came from Portsmouth, Va. Stebney is thirty-four years of age, medium size, mulatto, and quite wide awake. He was owned by an oysterman by the name of Jos. Carter, who lived near Portsmouth. Naturally enough his master "drank hard, gambled" extensively, and in every other respect was a very ordinary man. Nevertheless, he "owned twenty-five head," and had a wife and six children. Stebney testified that he had not been used hard, though he had been on the "auction-block three times." Left because he was "tired of being a servant." Armed with a broad-axe and hatchet, he started, joined by the above-named companions, and came in a skiff, by sea. Robert Lee was the brave Captain engaged to pilot this Slavery-sick party from the prison-house of bondage. And although every rod of rowing was attended with inconceivable peril, the desired haven was safely reached, and the overjoyed voyagers conducted to the Vigilance Committee.

JOHN is about forty years of age, and so near white that a microscope would be required to discern his colored origin. His father was white, and his mother nearly so. He also had been owned by the oysterman alluded to above; had been captain of one of his oyster-boats, until recently. And but for his attempt some months back to make his escape, he might have been this day in the care of his kind-hearted master. But, because of this wayward step on the part of John, his master felt called upon to humble him. Accordingly, the captaincy was taken from him, and he was compelled to struggle on in a less honorable position. Occasionally John's mind would be refreshed by his master relating the hard times in the North, the great starvation among the blacks, etc. He would also tell John how much better off he was as a "slave with a kind master to provide for all his wants," etc. Notwithstanding all this counsel, John did not rest contented until he was on the Underground Rail Road.

ROBERT was only nineteen, with an intelligent face and prepossessing manners; reads, writes and ciphers; and is about half Anglo-Saxon. He fled from Wm. H. Wilson, Esq., Cashier of the Virginia Bank. Until within the four years previous to Robert's escape, the cashier was spoken of as a "very good man;" but in consequence of speculations in a large Hotel in Portsmouth, and the then financial embarrassments, "he had become seriously involved," and decidedly changed in his manners. Robert noticed this, and concluded he had "better get out of danger as soon as possible."

ANTHONY and Isabella were an engaged couple, and desired to cast their lot where husband and wife could not be separated on the auction-block.

The following are of the Cambridge party, above alluded to. All left together, but for prudential reasons separated before reaching Philadelphia. The company that left Cambridge on the 24th of October may be thus recognized: Aaron Cornish and wife, with their six children; Solomon, George Anthony, Joseph, Edward James, Perry Lake, and a nameless babe, all very likely; Kit Anthony and wife Leah, and three children, Adam, Mary, and Murray; Joseph Hill and

Escaping from Norfolk in Capt. Lee's skiff.

wife Alice, and their son Henry; also Joseph's sister. Add to the above, Marshall Dutton and George Light, both single young men, and we have twenty-eight in one arrival, as hearty-looking, brave and interesting specimens of Slavery as could well be produced from Maryland. Before setting out they counted well the cost. Being aware that fifteen had left their neighborhood only a few days ahead of them, and that every slave-holder and slave-catcher throughout the community, were on the alert, and raging furiously against the inroads of the Underground Rail Road, they provided themselves with the following weapons of defense: three revolvers, three double-barreled pistols, three single-barreled pistols, three sword-canes, four butcher knives, one bowie-knife, and one paw.* Thus, fully resolved upon freedom or death, with scarcely provisions enough for a single day, while the rain and storm was piteously descending, fathers and mothers with children in their arms (Aaron Cornish had two)—the entire

---

*A paw is a weapon with iron prongs, four inches long, to be grasped with the hand and used in close encounter.

party started. Of course, their provisions gave out before they were fairly on the way, but not so with the storm. It continued to pour upon them for nearly three days. With nothing to appease the gnawings of hunger but parched corn and a few dry crackers, wet and cold, with several of the children sick, some of their feet bare and worn, and one of the mothers with an infant in her arms, incapable of partaking of the diet,—it is impossible to imagine the ordeal they were passing. It was enough to cause the bravest hearts to falter. But not for a moment did they allow themselves to look back. It was exceedingly agreeable to hear even the little children testify that in the most trying hour on the road, not for a moment did they want to go back. The following advertisement, taken from *The Cambridge Democrat* of November 4, shows how the Rev. Levi Traverse felt about Aaron—

> $300 REWARD.—Ran away from the subscriber, from the neighborhood of Town Point, on Saturday night, the 24th inst., my negro man, AARON CORNISH, about 35 years old. He is about five feet ten inches high, black, good-looking, rather pleasant countenance, and carries himself with a confident manner. He went off with his wife, DAFFNEY, a negro woman belonging to Reuben E. Phillips. I will give the above reward if taken out of the county, and $200 if taken in the county; in either case to be lodged in Cambridge Jail.
>
> October 25, 1857.
>
> LEVI D. TRAVERSE.

To fully understand the Rev. Mr. Traverse's authority for taking the liberty he did with Aaron's good name, it may not be amiss to give briefly a paragraph of private information from Aaron, relative to his master. The Rev. Mr. Traverse belonged to the Methodist Church, and was described by Aaron as a "bad young man; rattle-brained; with the appearance of not having good sense,—not enough to manage the great amount of property (he had been left wealthy) in his possession." Aaron's servitude commenced under this spiritual protector in May prior to the escape, immediately after the death of his old master. His deceased master, William D. Traverse, by the way, was the father-in-law, and at the same time own uncle of Aaron's reverend owner. Though the young master, for marrying his own cousin and uncle's daughter, had been for years the subject of the old gentle-man's wrath, and was not allowed to come near his house, or to enter-tain any reasonable hope of getting any of his father-in-law's estate, nevertheless, scarcely had the old man breathed his last, ere the young preacher seized upon the inheritance, slaves and all; at least he claimed two-thirds, allowing for the widow one-third. Unhesitatingly he had taken possession of all the slaves (some thirty head), and was making them feel his power to the fullest extent. To Aaron this in-creased oppression was exceedingly crushing, as he had been hoping at the death of his old master to be free. Indeed, it was understood that the old man had his will made, and freedom provided for the slaves. But, strangely enough, at his death no will could be found. Aaron was firmly of the conviction that the Rev. Mr. Traverse knew what became of it. Between the widow and the son-in-law, in conse-quence of his aggressive steps, existed much hostility, which strongly indicated the approach of a law-suit; therefore, except by escaping, Aaron could not see the faintest hope of freedom. Under his old mas-ter, the favor of hiring his time had been granted him. He had also been allowed by his wife's mistress (Miss Jane Carter, of Baltimore), to have his wife and children home with him—that is, until his chil-dren would grow to the age of eight and ten years, then they would be taken away and hired out at twelve or fifteen dollars a year at first. Her oldest boy, sixteen, hired the year he left for forty dollars. They had had ten children; two had died, two they were compelled to leave in chains; the rest they brought away. Not one dollar's expense had they been to their mistress. The industrious Aaron not only had to pay his own hire, but was obliged to do enough over-work to support his large family.

Though he said he had no special complaint to make against his old master, through whom he, with the rest of the slaves, hoped to ob-tain freedom, Aaron, nevertheless, spoke of him as a man of violent temper, severe on his slaves, drinking hard, etc., though he was a man of wealth and stood high in the community. One of Aaron's brothers, and others, had been sold South by him. It was on account of his in-veterate hatred of his son-in-law, who, he declared, should never have his property (having no other heir but his niece, except his widow), that the slaves relied on his promise to free them. Thus, in view of the facts referred to, Aaron was led to commit the unpardonable sin of running away with his wife Daffney, who, by the way, looked like a woman fully capable of taking care of herself and children, instead of having them stolen away from her, as though they were pigs.

JOSEPH VINEY and family—Joseph was "held to service or labor," by Charles Bryant, of Alexandria, Va. Joseph had very nearly finished paying for himself. His wife and children were held by Samuel Pattison, Esq., a member of the Methodist Church, "a great big man," "with red eyes, bald head, drank pretty freely," and in the language of Joseph, "wouldn't bear nothing." Two of Joseph's brothers-in-law had been sold by his master. Against Mrs. Pattison his complaint was, that "she was mean, sneaking, and did not want to give half enough to eat."

For the enlightenment of all Christendom, and coming posterity especially, the following advertisement and letter are recorded, with the hope that they will have an important historical value. The writer was at great pains to obtain these interesting documents, directly after the arrival of the memorable Twenty-Eight; and shortly afterwards furnished to the New York *Tribune*, in a prudential manner, a brief sketch of these very passengers, including the advertisements, but not the letter. It was safely laid away for history—

$2,000 REWARD.—Ran away from the subscriber on Saturday night, the 24th inst, FOURTEEN HEAD OF NEGROES, viz: Four men, two women, one boy and seven children. KIT is about 35 years of age, five feet six or seven inches high, dark chestnut color, and has a scar on one of his thumbs. JOE is about 30 years old, very black, his teeth are very white, and is about five feet eight inches high. HENRY is about 22 years old, five feet ten inches high, of dark chestnut color and large front teeth. JOE is about 20 years old, about five feet six inches high, heavy built and black. TOM is about 16 years old, about five feet high, light chestnut color. SUSAN is about 35 years old, dark chestnut color, and rather stout built; speaks rather slow, and has with her FOUR CHILDREN, varying from one to seven years of age. LEAH is about 28 years old, about five feet high, dark chestnut color, with

THREE CHILDREN, two boys and one girl, from one to eight years old.

I will give $1,000 if taken in the county, $1,500 if taken out of the county and in the State, and $2,000 if taken out of the State; in either case to be lodged in Cambridge (Md.) Jail, so that I can get them again; or I will give a fair proportion of the above reward if any part be secured.

October 26, 1857.

SAMUEL PATTISON,
Near Cambridge, Md.

P. S.—Since writing the above, I have discovered that my negro woman, SARAH JANE, 25 years old, stout built and chestnut color, has also run off.

S. P.

SAMUEL PATTISON'S LETTER.

CAMBRIDGE, Nov. 16th, 1857.

L. W. THOMPSON:—SIR, this morning I received your letter wishing an accurate description of my Negroes which ran away on the 24th of last month and the amt of reward offered &c &c. The description is as follows. *Kit* is about 35 years old, five feet, six or seven inches high, dark chestnut color and has a scar on one of his thumbs, he has a very quick step and walks very straight, and can read and write. *Joe,* is about 30 years old, very black and about five feet eight inches high, has a very pleasing appearance, he has a free wife who left with him she is a light molatoo, she has a child not over one year old. *Henry* is about 22 years old, five feet, ten inches high, of dark chestnut coller and large front teeth, he stoops a little in his walk and has a downward look. *Joe* is about 20 years old, about five feet six inches high, heavy built, and has a grum look and voice dull, and black. *Tom* is about 16 years old about five feet high light chestnut coller, smart active boy, and swagers in his walk. Susan is about 35 years old, dark chestnut coller and stout built, speaks rather slow and has with her *four children, three boys* and one *girl*—the girl has a thumb or finger on her left hand (part of it) cut off, the children are from 9 months to 8 years old. (the youngest a boy 9 months and the oldest whose name is Lloyd is about 8 years old) The husband of Susan (Joe Viney) started off with her, he is a slave, belonging to a gentleman in Alexandria D. C. he is about 40 years old and dark chestnut coller rather slender built and about five feet seven or eight inches high, he is also the Father of Henry, Joe and Tom. A *reward* of $400. will be given for his apprehension. *Leah* is about 28 years old about five feet high dark chestnut coller, with three children. 2 Boys and 1 girl, they are from one to eight years old, the oldest boy is called Adam, Leah is the wife of Kit, the first named man in the list. *Sarah Jane* is about 25 years old, stout built and chestnut coller, quick and active in her walk. Making in all 15 head, men, women and children belonging to me, or 16 head including Joe Viney, the husband of my woman Susan.

A *Reward* of $2250. will be given for my negroes if taken out of the State of Maryland and lodged in Cambridge or Baltimore Jail, so that I can get them or a fair proportion for any part of them. And including Joe Viney's reward $2650.00.

At the same time eight other negroes belonging to a neighbor of mine ran off, for which a reward of $1400.00 has been offered for them.

If you should want any information, witnesses to prove or identify the negroes, write immediately on to me. Or if you should need any information with regard to proving the negroes, before I could reach Philadelphia, you can call on Mr. Burroughs at Martin & Smith's store, Market Street, No 308. Phila and he can refer you to a gentleman who knows the negroes.

YOURS &C SAML. PATTISON.

This letter was in answer to one written in Philadelphia and signed, "L. W. Thompson." It is not improbable that Mr. Pattison's loss had produced such a high state of mental excitement that he was hardly in a condition for cool reflection, or he would have weighed the matter a little more carefully before exposing himself to the U. G. R. R. agents. But the letter possesses two commendable features, nevertheless. It was tolerably well written and prompt.

Here is a wonderful exhibition of affection for his contented and happy negroes. Whether Mr. Pattison suspended on suddenly learning that he was minus fifteen head, the writer cannot say. But that there was a great slave hunt in every direction there is no room to doubt. Though much more might be said about the parties concerned, it must suffice to add that they came to the Vigilance Committee in a very sad plight—in tattered garments, hungry, sick, and penniless; but they were kindly clothed, fed, doctored, and sent on their way rejoicing.

DANIEL STANLY, Nat Amby, John Scott, Hannah Peters, Henrietta Dobson, Elizabeth Amby, Josiah Stanly, Caroline Stanly, Daniel Stanly, jr., John Stanly and Miller Stanly (arrival from Cambridge.) Daniel is about 35, well-made and wide-awake. Fortunately, in emancipating himself, he also, through great perseverance, secured the freedom of his wife and six children; one child he was compelled to leave behind. Daniel belonged to Robert Calender, a farmer, and, "except when in a passion," said to be "pretty clever." However, considering as a father, that it was his "duty to do all he could" for his children, and that all work and no play makes Jack a dull boy, Daniel felt bound to seek refuge in Canada. His wife and children were owned by "Samuel Count, an old, bald-headed, bad man," who "had of late years been selling and buying slaves as a business," though he stood high and was a "big bug in Cambridge." The children were truly likely-looking.

Nat is no ordinary man. Like a certain other Nat known to history, his honest and independent bearing in every respect was that of a natural hero. He was full black, and about six feet high; of powerful physical proportions, and of more than ordinary intellectual capacities. With the strongest desire to make the Port of Canada safely, he had resolved to be "carried back," if attacked by the slave hunters, "only as a dead man." He was held to service by John Muir, a wealthy farmer, and the owner of 40 or 50 slaves. "Muir would drink and was generally devilish." Two of Nat's sisters and one of his brothers had been "sold away to Georgia by him." Therefore, admonished by threats and fears of having to pass through the same fiery furnace, Nat was led to consider the U. G. R. R. scheme. It was through the

Twenty-eight fugitives escaping from the eastern shore of Maryland.

marriage of Nat's mistress to his present owner that he came into Muir's hands. "Up to the time of her death," he had been encouraged to "hope" that he would be "free;" indeed, he was assured by her "dying testimony that the slaves were not to be sold." But regardless of the promises and will of his departed wife, Muir soon extinguished all hopes of freedom from that quarter. But not believing that God had put one man here to "be the servant of another—to work," and get none of the benefit of his labor, Nat armed himself with a good pistol and a big knife, and taking his wife with him, bade adieu forever to bondage. Observing that Lizzie (Nat's wife) looked pretty decided and resolute, a member of the committee remarked, "Would your wife fight for freedom?" "I have heard her say she would wade through blood and tears for her freedom," said Nat, in the most serious mood.

The following advertisement from *The Cambridge Democrat* of Nov. 4, speaks for itself—

$300 REWARD.—Ran away from the subscriber, on Saturday night last, 17th inst., my negro woman Lizzie, about 28 years old. She is medium sized, dark complexion, good-looking, with rather a down look. When spoken to, replies quickly. She was well dressed, wearing a red and green blanket shawl, and carried with her a variety of clothing. She ran off in company with her husband, Nat Amby (belonging to John Muir, Esq.), who is about 6 feet in height, with slight impediment in his speech, dark chestnut color, and a large scar on the side of his neck.

I will give the above reward if taken in this County, or one-half of what she sells for if taken out of the County or State. In either case to be lodged in Cambridge Jail.

Cambridge, Oct. 21, 1857.

ALEXANDER H. BAYLY.

P. S.—For the apprehension of the above-named negro man Nat, and delivery in Cambridge Jail, I will give $500 reward.

JOHN MUIR.

Now since Nat's master has been introduced in the above order, it seems but appropriate that Nat should be heard too; consequently the following letter is inserted for what it is worth:

AUBURN, June 10th, 1858.

MR. WILLIAM STILL:—Sir, will you be so Kind as to write a letter to affey White in straw berry alley in Baltimore city on the point Say to her at nat Ambey that I wish to Know from her the Last Letar that Joseph Ambie and Henry Ambie two Brothers and Ann Warfield a cousin of them two boys I state above I would like to hear from my mother sichy Ambie you will Please write to my mother and tell her that I am well and doing well and state to her that I perform my Relissius dutys and I would like to hear from her and want to know if she is performing her Relissius dutys yet and send me word from all her children I left behind say to affey White that I wish her to write me a Letter in Hast my wife is well and doing well and my nephew is doing well Please tell affey White when she writes to me to Let me know where Joseph and Henry Ambie is

Mr. Still Please Look on your Book and you will find my name on your Book They was eleven of us children and all when we came through and I feal interrested about my Brothers I have never heard from them since I Left home you will Please Be Kind annough to attend to this Letter When you send the answer to this Letter you will Please send it to P. R. Freeman Auburn City Cayuga County New York

Yours Truly   NAT AMBIE.

WILLIAM is 25, complexion brown, intellect naturally good, with no favorable notions of the peculiar institution. He was armed with a formidable dirk-knife, and declared he would use it if attacked, rather than be dragged back to bondage.

HANNAH is a hearty-looking young woman of 23 or 24, with a countenance that indicated that liberty was what she wanted and was contending for, and that she could not willingly submit to the yoke. Though she came with the Cambridge party, she did not come from Cambridge, but from Marshall Hope, Caroline County, where she had been owned by Charles Peters, a man who had distinguished himself by getting "drunk, scratching and fighting, etc.," not unfrequently in his own family even. She had no parents that she knew of. Left because they used her "so bad, beat and knocked" her about.

"JACK SCOTT." Jack is about thirty-six years of age, substantially built, dark color, and of quiet and prepossessing manners. He was owned by David B. Turner, Esq., a dry goods merchant of New York. By birth, Turner was a Virginian, and a regular slave-holder. His slaves were kept hired out by the year. As Jack had had but slight acquaintance with his New York owner, he says but very little about him. He was moved to leave simply because he had got tired of working for the "white people for nothing." Fled from Richmond, Va. Jack went to Canada direct. The following letter furnishes a clew to his whereabouts, plans, etc.

MONTREAL, September 1st 1859.

DEAR SIR:—It is with extreme pleasure that I set down to inclose you a few lines to let you know that I am well & I hope when these few lines come to hand they may find you & your family in good health and prosperity I left your house Nov. 3d, 1857, for Canada I Received a letter here from James Carter in Peters burg, saying that my wife would leave there about the 28th or the first September and that he would send her on by way of Philadelphia to you to send on to Montreal if she come on you be please to send her on and as there is so many boats coming here all times a day I may not know what time she will. So you be please to give her this direction, she can get a cab and go to the Donegana Hotel and Edmund Turner is there he will take you where I lives and if he is not there cabman take you to Mr. Taylors on Durham St. nearly opposite to the Methodist Church. Nothing more at present but Remain your well wisher

JOHN SCOTT.

C. HITCHENS.—This individual took his departure from Milford, Del., where he was owned by Wm. Hill, a farmer, who took special delight in having "fighting done on the place." This passenger was one of our least intelligent travelers. He was about 22.

MAJOR ROSS.—Major fled from John Jay, a farmer residing in the neighborhood of Havre de Grace, Md. But for the mean treatment received from Mr. Jay, Major might have been foolish enough to have remained all his days in chains. "It's an ill wind that blows nobody any good."

HENRY OBERNE.—Henry was to be free at 28, but preferred having it at 21, especially as he was not certain that 28 would ever come. He is of chestnut color, well made, &c., and came from Seaford, Md.

PERRY BURTON.—Perry is about twenty-seven years of age, decidedly colored, medium size, and only of ordinary intellect. He acknowledged John R. Burton, a farmer on Indian River, as his master, and escaped because he wanted "some day for himself."

ALFRED HUBERT, Israel Whitney and John Thompson. Alfred is of powerful muscular appearance and naturally of a good intellect. He is full dark chestnut color, and would doubtless fetch a high price. He was owned by Mrs. Matilda Niles, from whom he had hired his time, paying $110 yearly. He had no fault to find with his mistress, except he observed she had a young family growing up, into whose hands he feared he might unluckily fall some day, and saw no way of avoiding it but by flight. Being only twenty-eight, he may yet make his mark.

ISRAEL was owned by Elijah Money. All that he could say in favor of his master was, that he treated him "respectfully," though he "drank hard." Israel was about thirty-six, and another excellent specimen of an able-bodied and wide-awake man. He hired his time at the rate of $120 a year, and had to find his wife and child in the bargain. He came from Alexandria, Va.

INTERESTING LETTER FROM ISRAEL.

HAMILTON, Oct. 16, 1858.

WILLIAM STILL—*My Dear Friend:*—I saw Carter and his friend a few days ago, and they told me, that you was well. On the seventh of October my wife came to Hamilton. Mr. A. Hurberd, who came from Virginia with me, is going to get married the 20th of November, next. I wish you would write to me how many of my friends you have seen since October, 1857. Montgomery Green keeps a barber shop in Cayuga, in the State of New York. I have not heard of Oscar Ball but once since I came here, and then he was well and doing well. George Carroll is in Hamilton. The times are very dull at present, and have been ever since I came here. Please write soon. Nothing more at present, only I still remain in Hamilton, C. W.

ISRAEL WHITNEY.

JOHN is nineteen years of age, mulatto, spare made, but not lacking in courage, mother wit or perseverance. He was born in Fauquier county, Va., and, after experiencing Slavery for a number of years there—being sold two or three times to the "highest bidder"—he was finally purchased by a cotton planter named Hezekiah Thompson, residing at Huntsville, Alabama. Immediately after the sale Hezekiah bundled his new "purchase" off to Alabama, where he succeeded in keeping him only about two years, for at the end of that time John determined to strike a blow for liberty. The incentive to this step was the inhuman treatment he was subjected to. Cruel indeed did he find it there. His master was a young man, "fond of drinking and carousing, and always ready for a fight or a knock-down." A short time before John left his master whipped him so severely with the "bull whip" that he could not use his arm for three or four days. Seeing but one way of escape (and that more perilous than the way William and Ellen Craft, or Henry Box Brown traveled), he resolved to try it. It was to get on the top of the car, instead of inside of it, and thus ride of nights, till nearly daylight, when, at a stopping-place on the road, he would slip off the car, and conceal himself in the woods until under cover of the next night he could manage to get on the top of another car. By this most hazardous mode of travel he reached Virginia.

It may be best not to attempt to describe how he suffered at the hands of his owners in Alabama; or how severely he was pinched with hunger in traveling; or how, when he reached his old neighborhood in Virginia, he could not venture to inquire for his mother, brothers or sisters, to receive from them an affectionate word, an encouraging smile, a crust of bread, or a drink of water.

Success attended his efforts for more than two weeks; but alas, after having got back north of Richmond, on his way home to Alexandria, he was captured and put in prison; his master being informed of the fact, came on and took possession of him again. At first he refused to sell him; said he "had money enough and owned about thirty slaves;" therefore wished to "take him back to make an example of him." However, through the persuasion of an uncle of his, he consented to sell. Accordingly, John was put on the auction-block and bought for $1,300 by Green McMurray, a regular trader in Richmond. McMurray again offered him for sale, but in consequence of hard times and the high price demanded, John did not go off, at least not in the way the trader desired to dispose of him, but did, nevertheless, succeed in going off on the Underground Rail Road. Thus once more he reached his old home, Alexandria. His mother was in one place, and his six brothers and sisters evidently scattered, where he knew not. Since he was five years of age, not one of them had he seen.

If such sufferings and trials were not entitled to claim for the sufferer the honor of a hero, where in all Christendom could one be found who could prove a better title to that appellation?

It is needless to say that the Committee extended to him brotherly kindness, sympathized with him deeply, and sent him on his way rejoicing.

Of his subsequent career the following extract from a letter written at London shows that he found no rest for the soles of his feet under the Stars and Stripes in New York:

> I hope that you will remember John Thompson, who passed through your hands, I think, in October, 1857, at the same time that Mr. Cooper, from Charleston, South Carolina, came on. I was engaged at New York, in the barber business, with a friend, and was doing very well, when I was betrayed and obliged to sail for England very suddenly, my master being in the city to arrest me. (LONDON, December 21st, 1860.)

JEREMIAH COLBURN.—Jeremiah is a bright mulatto, of prepossessing appearance, reads and writes, and is quite intelligent. He fled from Charleston, where he had been owned by Mrs. E. Williamson, an old lady about seventy-five, a member of the Episcopal Church, and opposed to Freedom. As far as he was concerned, however, he said, she had treated him well; but, knowing that the old lady would not be long here, he judged it was best to look out in time. Consequently, he availed himself of an Underground Rail Road ticket, and bade adieu to that hot-bed of secession, South Carolina. Indeed, he was fair enough to pass for white, and actually came the entire journey from Charleston to this city under the garb of a white gentleman. With regard to gentlemanly bearing, however, he was all right in this particular. Nevertheless, as he had been a slave all his days, he found that it required no small amount of nerve to succeed in running the gauntlet with slave-holders and slave-catchers for so long a journey.

The following pointed epistle, from Jeremiah Colburn alias William Cooper, beautifully illustrates the effects of Freedom on many a passenger who received hospitalities at the Philadelphia depot—

SYRACUSE, June 9th, 1858.

MR. STILL:—*Dear Sir:*—One of your Underground R. R. Passenger Drop you these few Lines to let you see that he have not forgotten you one who have Done so much for him well sir I am still in Syracuse, well in regard to what I am Doing for a Living I no you would like to hear, I am in the Painting Business, and have as much at that as I can do, and enough to Last me all the Summer, I had a knolledge of Painting Before I left the South, the Hotell where I was working Last winter the Proprietor fail & shot up in the Spring and I Loose evry thing that I was working for all Last winter. I have Ritten a Letter to my Friend P. Christianson some time a goo & have never Received an Answer, I hope this wont Be the case with this one, I have an idea sir, next winter iff I can this summer make Enough to Pay Expenses, to goo to that school at McGrowville & spend my winter their. I am going sir to try to Prepair myself for a Lectuer, I am going sir By the Help of god to try and Do something for the Caus to help my Poor Breathern that are suffering under the yoke. Do give my Respect to Mrs Stills & Perticular to Miss Julia Kelly, I suppose she is still with you yet, I am in great hast you must excuse my short letter. I hope these few Lines may fine you as they Leave me quite well. It will afford me much Pleasure to hear from you.

yours Truly,   WILLIAM COOPER.

John Thompson is still here and Doing well.

It will be seen that this young Charlestonian had rather exalted notions in his head. He was contemplating going to McGrawville College, for the purpose of preparing himself for the lecturing field. Was it not rather strange that he did not want to return to his "kind-hearted old mistress?"

THOMAS HENRY, NATHAN COLLINS AND HIS WIFE MARY ELLEN.—Thomas is about twenty-six, quite dark, rather of a raw-boned make, indicating that times with him had been other than smooth. A certain Josiah Wilson owned Thomas. He was a cross, rugged man, allowing not half enough to eat, and worked his slaves late and early. Especially within the last two or three months previous to the escape, he had been intensely savage, in consequence of having lost, not long before, two of his servants. Ever since that misfortune, he had frequently talked of "putting the rest in his pocket." This distressing threat made the rest love him none the more; but, to make assurances doubly sure, after giving them their supper every evening, which consisted of delicious "skimmed milk, corn cake and a herring each," he would very carefully send them up in the loft over the kitchen, and there "lock them up," to remain until called the next morning at three or four o'clock to go to work again. Destitute of money, clothing, and a knowledge of the way, situated as they were they concluded to make an effort for Canada.

NATHAN was also a fellow-servant with Thomas, and of course owned by Wilson. Nathan's wife, however, was owned by Wilson's son, Abram. Nathan was about twenty-five years of age, not very dark. He had a remarkably large head on his shoulders and was the picture of determination, and apparently was exactly the kind of a subject that might be desirable in the British possessions, in the forest or on the farm.

His wife, Mary Ellen, is a brown-skinned, country-looking young woman, about twenty years of age. In escaping, they had to break jail, in the dead of night, while all were asleep in the big house; and thus they succeeded. What Mr. Wilson did, said or thought about these "shiftless" creatures we are not prepared to say; we may, notwithstanding, reasonably infer that the Underground has come in for a liberal share of his indignation and wrath. The above travelers came from near New Market, Md. The few rags they were clad in were not really worth the price that a woman would ask for washing them, yet they brought with them about all they had. Thus they had to be newly rigged at the expense of the Vigilance Committee.

The Cambridge Democrat, of Nov. 4, 1857, from which the advertisements were cut, said—

> "At a meeting of the people of this county, held in Cambridge, on the 2d of November, to take into consideration the better protection of the interests of the slave-owners; among other things that were done, it was resolved to enforce the various acts of Assembly * * * * relating to servants and slaves.
>
> "The act of 1715, chap. 44, sec. 2, provides 'that from and after the publication thereof no servant or servants whatsoever, within this province, whether by indenture or by the custom of the counties, or hired for wages shall travel by land or water ten miles from the house of his, her or their master, mistress or dame, without a note under

their hands, or under the hands of his, her or their overseer, if any be, under the penalty of being taken for a runaway, and to suffer such penalties as hereafter provided against runaways.' The Act of 1806, chap. 81, sec. 5, provides, 'That any person taking up such runaway, shall have and receive $6,' to be paid by the master or owner. It was also determined to have put in force the act of 1825, chap. 161, and the act of 1839, chap. 320, relative to idle, vagabond, free negroes, providing for their sale or banishment from the State. All persons interested, are hereby notified that the aforesaid laws, in particular, will be enforced, and all officers failing to enforce them will be presented to the Grand Jury, and those who desire to avoid the penalties of the aforesaid statutes are requested to conform to these provisions."

As to the modus operandi by which so many men, women and children were delivered and safely forwarded to Canada, despite slave-hunters and the fugitive slave law, the subjoined letters, from different agents and depots, will throw important light on the question.

Men and women aided in this cause who were influenced by no oath of secrecy, who received not a farthing for their labors, who believed that God had put it into the hearts of all mankind to love liberty, and had commanded men to "feel for those in bonds as bound with them," "to break every yoke and let the oppressed go free." But here are the letters, bearing at least on some of the travelers:

WILMINGTON, 10th Mo. 31st, 1857.

ESTEEMED FRIEND WILLIAM STILL:—I write to inform thee that we have either 17 or 27, I am not certain which, of that large Gang of God's poor, and I hope they are safe. The man who has them in charge informed me there were 27 safe and one boy lost during last night, about 14 years of age, without shoes; we have felt some anxiety about him, for fear he may be taken up and betray the rest. I have since been informed there are but 17 so that I cannot at present tell which is correct. I have several looking out for the lad; they will be kept from Phila. for the present. My principal object in writing thee at this time is to inform thee of what one of our constables told me this morning; he told me that a colored man in Phila. who professed to be a great friend of the colored people was a traitor; that he had been written to by an Abolitionist in Baltimore, to keep a look out for those slaves that left Cambridge this night week, told him they would be likely to pass through Wilmington on 6th day or 7th day night, and the colored man in Phila. had written to the master of part of them telling him the above, and the master arrived here yesterday in consequence of the information, and told one of our constables the above; the man told the name of the Baltimore writer, which he had forgotten, but declined telling the name of the colored man in Phila. I hope you will be able to find out who he is, and should I be able to learn the name of the Baltimore friend, I will put him on his Guard, respecting his Phila. correspondents. As ever thy friend, and the friend of Humanity, without regard to color or clime.

THOS. GARRETT.

How much truth there was in the "constable's" story to the effect, "that a colored man in Philadelphia, who professed to be a great friend of the colored people, was a traitor, etc.," the Committee never learned. As a general thing, colored people were true to the fugitive slave; but now and then some unprincipled individuals, under various pretenses, would cause us great anxiety.

LETTER FROM JOHN AUGUSTA.

NORRISTOWN Oct 18th 1857 2 o'clock P M

DEAR SIR:—There is Six men and women and Five children making Eleven Persons. If you are willing to Receve them write to me imediately and I will bring them to your To morrow Evening I would not Have wrote this But the Times are so much worse Financialy that I thought It best to hear From you Before I Brought such a Crowd Down Pleas Answer this and

Oblige JOHN AUGUSTA.

This document has somewhat of a military appearance about it. It is short and to the point. Friend Augusta was well known in Norristown as a first-rate hair-dresser and a prompt and trustworthy Underground Rail Road agent. Of course a speedy answer was returned to his note, and he was instructed to bring the eleven passengers on to the Committee in Brotherly Love.

LETTER FROM MISS G. LEWIS ABOUT A PORTION OF THE SAME "MEMORABLE TWENTY-EIGHT."

SUNNYSIDE, Nov. 6th, 1857.

DEAR FRIEND:—Eight more of the large company reached our place last night, direct from Ercildown. The eight constitute one family of them, the husband and wife with four children under eight years of age, wish tickets for Elmira. Three sons, nearly grown, will be forwarded to Phila., probably by the train which passes Phœnixville at seven o'clock of to-morrow evening the seventh. It would be safest to meet them there. We shall send them to Elijah with the request for them to be sent there. And I presume they will be. If they should not arrive you may suppose it did not suit Elijah to send them.

We will send the money for the tickets by C. C. Burleigh, who will be in Phila. on second day morning. If you please, you will forward the tickets by to-morrow's mail as we do not have a mail again till third day. Yours hastily,

G. LEWIS.

Please give directions for forwarding to Elmira and name the price of tickets.

At first Miss Lewis thought of forwarding only a part of her fugitive guests to the Committee in Philadelphia, but on further consideration, all were safely sent along in due time, and the Committee took great pains to have them made as comfortable as possible, as the cases of these mothers and children especially called forth the deepest sympathy.

In this connection it seems but fitting to allude to Captain Lee's sufferings on account of his having brought away in a skiff, by sea, a party of four, alluded to in the beginning of this single month's report.

Unfortunately he was suspected, arrested, tried, convicted, and torn from his wife and two little children, and sent to the Richmond Penitentiary for twenty-five years. Before being sent away from Portsmouth, Va., where he was tried, for ten days in succession in the prison five lashes a day were laid heavily on his bare back. The further sufferings of poor Lee and his heart-broken wife, and his little daughter and son, are too painful for minute recital. In this city the friends of Freedom did all in their power to comfort Mrs. Lee, and administered aid to her and her children; but she broke down under her mournful fate, and went to that bourne from whence no traveler ever returns.

Captain Lee suffered untold misery in prison, until he, also, not a great while before the Union forces took possession of Richmond, sank beneath the severity of his treatment, and went likewise to the grave. The two children for a long time were under the care of Mr. Wm. Ingram of Philadelphia, who voluntarily, from pure benevolence, proved himself to be a father and a friend to them. To their poor mother also he had been a true friend.

The way in which Captain Lee came to be convicted, if the Committee were correctly informed and they think they were, was substantially in this wise: In the darkness of the night, four men, two of them constables, one of the other two, the owner of one of the slaves who had been aided away by Lee, seized the wife of one of the fugitives and took her to the woods, where the fiends stripped every particle of clothing from her person, tied her to a tree, and armed with knives, cowhides and a shovel, swore vengeance against her, declaring they would kill her if she did not testify against Lee. At first she refused to reveal the secret; indeed she knew but little to reveal; but her savage tormentors beat her almost to death. Under this barbarous infliction she was constrained to implicate Captain Lee, which was about all the evidence the prosecution had against him. And in reality her evidence, for two reasons, should not have weighed a straw, as it was contrary to the laws of the State of Virginia, to admit the testimony of colored persons against white; then again for the reason that this testimony was obtained wholly by brute force.

But in this instance, this woman on whom the murderous attack had been made, was brought into court on Lee's trial and was bid to simply make her statement with regard to Lee's connection with the escape of her husband. This she did of course. And in the eyes of this chivalric court, this procedure "was all right." But thank God the events since those dark and dreadful days, afford abundant proof that the All-seeing Eye was not asleep to the daily sufferings of the poor bondman.

A Slave Girl's Narrative

CORDELIA LONEY, SLAVE OF MRS. JOSEPH CAHELL
(WIDOW OF THE LATE HON. JOSEPH CAHELL, OF VA.), OF
FREDERICKSBURG, VA.—CORDELIA'S ESCAPE FROM HER
MISTRESS IN PHILADELPHIA

⮑ Rarely did the peculiar institution present the relations of mistress and maid-servant in a light so apparently favorable as in the case of Mrs. Joseph Cahell (widow of the late Hon. Jos Cahell, of Va.), and her slave, Cordelia. The Vigilance Committee's first knowledge of either of these memorable personages was brought about in the following manner.

About the 30th of March, in the year 1859, a member of the Vigilance Committee was notified by a colored servant, living at a fashionable boardinghouse on Chestnut street that a lady with a slave woman from Fredericksburg, Va., was boarding at said house, and, that said slave woman desired to receive counsel and aid from the Committee, as she was anxious to secure her freedom, before her mistress returned to the South. On further consultation about the matter, a suitable hour was named for the meeting of the Committee and the Slave at the above named boarding-house. Finding that the woman was thoroughly reliable, the Committee told her "that two modes of deliverance were open before her. One was to take her trunk and all her clothing and quietly retire." The other was to "sue out a writ of habeas corpus, and bring the mistress before the Court, where she would be required, under the laws of Pennsylvania, to show cause why she restrained this woman of her freedom." Cordelia concluded to adopt the former expedient, provided the Committee would protect her. Without hesitation the Committee answered her, that to the extent of their ability, she should have their aid with pleasure, without delay. Consequently a member of the Committee was directed to be on hand at a given hour that evening, as Cordelia would certainly be ready to leave her mistress to take care of herself. Thus, at the appointed hour, Cordelia, very deliberately, accompanied the Committee away from her "kind hearted old mistress."

In the quiet and security of the Vigilance Committee Room, Cordelia related substantially the following brief story touching her relationship as a slave to Mrs. Joseph Cahell. In this case, as with thousands and tens of thousands of others, as the old adage fitly expresses it, "All is not gold that glitters." Under this apparently pious and noble-minded lady, it will be seen, that Cordelia had known naught but misery and sorrow.

Mrs. Cahell, having engaged board for a month at a fashionable private boarding-house on Chestnut street, took an early opportunity to caution Cordelia against going into the streets, and against having anything to say or do with "free niggers in particular"; withal, she appeared unusually kind, so much so, that before retiring to bed in the evening, she would call Cordelia to her chamber, and by her side would take her Prayer-book and Bible, and go through the forms of devotional service. She stood very high both as a church communicant and a lady in society.

For a fortnight it seemed as though her prayers were to be answered, for Cordelia apparently bore herself as submissively as ever, and Madame received calls and accepted invitations from some of the *elite* of the city, without suspecting any intention on the part of Cordelia to escape. But Cordelia could not forget how her children had all been sold by her mistress!

Cordelia was about fifty-seven years of age, with about an equal proportion of colored and white blood in her veins; very neat, respectful and prepossessing in manner.

From her birth to the hour of her escape she had worn the yoke under Mrs. C., as her most efficient and reliable maid-servant. She had been at her mistress' beck and call as seamstress, dressing-maid, nurse in the sickroom, etc., etc., under circumstances that might appear to the casual observer uncommonly favorable for a slave. Indeed, on his first interview with her, the Committee man was so forcibly impressed with the belief, that her condition in Virginia had been favorable, that he hesitated to ask her if she did not desire her liberty. A few moments' conversation with her, however, convinced him of her good sense and decision of purpose with regard to this matter. For, in answer to the first question he put to her, she answered, that "As many creature comforts and religious privileges as she had been the recipient of under her 'kind mistress,' still she 'wanted to be free,' and 'was bound to leave,' that she had been 'treated very cruelly;' that her children had 'all been sold away' from her; that she had been threatened with sale herself 'on the first insult,'" etc.

She was willing to take the entire responsibility of taking care of herself. On the suggestion of a friend, before leaving her mistress, she was disposed to sue for her freedom, but, upon a reconsideration of the matter, she chose rather to accept the hospitality of the Underground Rail Road, and leave in a quiet way and go to Canada, where she would be free indeed. Accordingly she left her mistress and was soon a free woman.

The following sad experience she related calmly, in the presence of several friends, an evening or two after she left her mistress:

Two sons and two daughters had been sold from her by her mistress, within the last three years, since the death of her master. Three of her children had been sold to the Richmond market and the other in Nelson county.

Paulina was the first sold, two years ago last May. Nat was the next; he was sold to Abram Warrick, of Richmond. Paulina was sold before it was named to her mother that it had entered her mistress's mind to dispose of her. Nancy, from infancy, had been in poor health. Nevertheless, she had been obliged to take her place in the field with the rest of the slaves, of more rugged constitution, until she had passed her twentieth year, and had become a mother. Under these circumstances, the overseer and his wife complained to the mistress that her health was really too bad for a field hand and begged that she might be taken where her duties would be less oppressive. Accordingly, she was withdrawn from the field, and was set to spinning and weaving. When too sick to work her mistress invariably took the ground, that "nothing was the matter," notwithstanding the fact, that her family physician, Dr. Ellsom, had pronounced her "quite weakly and sick."

In an angry mood one day, Mrs. Cahell declared she would cure her; and again sent her to the field, "with orders to the overseer, to whip her every day, and make her work or kill her." Again the overseer said it was "no use to try, for her health would not stand it," and she was forthwith returned. The mistress then concluded to sell her.

One Sabbath evening a nephew of hers, who resided in New Orleans, happened to be on a visit to his aunt, when it occurred to her, that she had "better get Nancy off if possible." Accordingly, Nancy was called in for examination. Being dressed in her "Sunday best" and "before a poor candle-light," she appeared to good advantage; and the nephew concluded to start with her on the following Tuesday morning. However, the next morning, he happened to see her by the light of the sun, and in her working garments, which satisfied him that he had been grossly deceived; that she would barely live to reach New Orleans; he positively refused to carry out the previous evening's contract, thus leaving her in the hands of her mistress, with the advice, that she should "doctor her up."

The mistress, not disposed to be defeated, obviated the difficulty by selecting a little boy, made a lot of the two, and thus made it an inducement to a purchaser to buy the sick woman; the boy and the woman brought $700.

In the sale of her children, Cordelia was as little regarded as if she had been a cow.

"I felt wretched," she said, with emphasis, "when I heard that Nancy had been sold," which was not until after she had been removed. "But," she continued, "I was not at liberty to make my grief known to a single white soul. I wept and couldn't help it." But remembering that she was liable, "on the first insult," to be sold herself, she sought no sympathy from her mistress, whom she describes as "a woman who shows as little kindness towards her servants as any woman in the States of America. She neither likes to feed nor clothe well."

With regard to flogging, however, in days past, she had been up to the mark. "A many a slap and blow" had Cordelia received since she arrived at womanhood, directly from the madam's own hand.

One day smarting under cruel treatment, she appealed to her mistress in the following strain: "I stood by your mother in all her sickness and nursed her till she died!" "I waited on your niece, night and day for months, till she died." "I waited upon your husband all my life—in his sickness especially, and shrouded him in death, etc., yet I am treated cruelly." It was of no avail.

Her mistress, at one time, was the owner of about five hundred slaves, but within the last few years she had greatly lessened the number by sales.

She stood very high as a lady, and was a member of the Episcopal Church.

To punish Cordelia, on several occasions, she had been sent to one of the plantations to work as a field hand. Fortunately, however, she found the overseers more compassionate than her mistress, though she received no particular favors from any of them.

Asking her to name the overseers, etc., she did so. The first was "Marks, a thin-visaged, poor-looking man, great for swearing." The second was "Gilbert Brower, a very rash, portly man." The third was "Buck Young, a stout man, and very sharp." The fourth was "Lynn Powell, a tall man with red whiskers, very contrary and spiteful." There was also a fifth one, but his name was lost.

Thus Cordelia's experience, though chiefly confined to the "great house," extended occasionally over the corn and tobacco fields, among the overseers and field hands generally. But under no circumstances could she find it in her heart to be thankful for the privileges of Slavery.

After leaving her mistress she learned, with no little degree of pleasure, that a perplexed state of things existed at the boarding-house; that her mistress was seriously puzzled to imagine how she would get her shoes and stockings on and off; how she would get her head combed, get dressed, be attended to in sickness, etc., as she (Cordelia), had been compelled to discharge these offices all her life.

Most of the boarders, being slave-holders, naturally sympathized in her affliction; and some of them went so far as to offer a reward to some of the colored servants to gain a knowledge of her whereabouts. Some charged the servants with having a hand in her leaving, but all agreed that "she had left a very kind and indulgent mistress," and had acted very foolishly in running out of Slavery into Freedom.

A certain Doctor of Divinity, the pastor of an Episcopal church in this city and a friend of the mistress, hearing of her distress, by request or voluntarily, undertook to find out Cordelia's place of seclusion. Hailing on the street a certain colored man with a familiar face, who he thought knew nearly all the colored people about town, he related to him the predicament of his lady friend from the South, remarked how kindly she had always treated her servants, signified that Cordelia would rue the change, and be left to suffer among the "miserable blacks down town," that she would not be able to take care of herself; quoted Scripture justifying Slavery, and finally suggested that he (the colored man) would be doing a duty and a kindness to the fugitive by using his influence to "find her and prevail upon her to return."

It so happened that the colored man thus addressed, was Thomas Dorsey, the well-known fashionable caterer of Philadelphia, who had had the experience of quite a number of years as a slave at the South,—had himself once been pursued as a fugitive, and having, by his industry in the condition of Freedom, acquired a handsome estate, he felt entirely qualified to reply to the reverend gentleman, which he did, though in not very respectful phrases, telling him that Cordelia had as good a right to her liberty as he had, or her mistress either; that God had never intended one man to be the slave of another; that it was all false about the slaves being better off than the free colored people; that he would find as many "poor, miserably degraded," of his own color "down-town," as among the "degraded blacks"; and concluded by telling him that he would "rather give her a hundred dollars to help her off, than to do aught to make known her whereabouts, if he knew ever so much about her."

What further steps were taken by the discomfited divine, the mistress, or her boarding-house sympathizers, the Committee was not informed.

But with regard to Cordelia: she took her departure for Canada, in the midst of the Daniel Webster (fugitive) trial, with the hope of being permitted to enjoy the remainder of her life in Freedom and peace. Being a member of the Baptist Church, and professing to be a Christian, she was persuaded that, by industry and assistance of the Lord, a way would be opened to the seeker of Freedom even in a strange land and among strangers.

This story appeared in part in the *N. Y. Evening Post,* having been furnished by the writer, without his name to it. It is certainly none the less interesting now, as it may be read in the light of Universal Emancipation.

Barnaby Grigby, Alias John Boyer, and Mary Elizabeth, His Wife; Frank Wanzer, Alias Robert Scott; Emily Foster, Alias Ann Wood

(TWO OTHERS WHO STARTED WITH THEM
WERE CAPTURED)

⊂⊒ All these persons journeyed together from Loudon Co., Va. on horseback and in a carriage for more than one hundred miles. Availing themselves of a holiday and their master's horses and carriage, they as deliberately started for Canada, as though they had never been taught that it was their duty, as servants, to "obey their masters." In this particular showing a most utter disregard of the interest of their "kind-hearted and indulgent owners." They left home on Monday, Christmas Eve, 1855, under the leadership of Frank Wanzer, and arrived in Columbia the following Wednesday at one o'clock. As willfully as they had thus made their way along, they had not found it smooth sailing by any means. The biting frost and snow rendered their travel anything but agreeable. Nor did they escape the gnawings of hunger, traveling day and night. And whilst these "articles" were in the very act of running away with themselves and their kind master's best horses and carriage—when about one hundred miles from home, in the neighborhood of Cheat river, Maryland, they were attacked by "six white men, and a boy," who, doubtless, supposing that their intentions were of a "wicked and unlawful character" felt it to be their duty in kindness to their masters, if not to the travelers to demand of them an account of themselves. In other words, the assailants posi-

A bold stroke for freedom.

tively commanded the fugitives to "show what right" they possessed, to be found in a condition apparently so unwarranted.

The *spokesman* amongst the fugitives, affecting no ordinary amount of dignity, told their assailants plainly, that "no gentleman would interfere with persons riding along civilly"—not allowing it to be supposed that they were slaves, of course. These "gentlemen," however, were not willing to accept this account of the travelers, as their very decided steps indicated. Having the law on their side, they were for compelling the fugitives to surrender without further parley.

At this juncture, the fugitives verily believing that the time had arrived for the practical use of their pistols and dirks, pulled them out of their concealment—the young women as well as the young men—and declared they would not be "taken!" One of the white men raised his gun, pointing the muzzle directly towards one of the young women, with the threat that he would "shoot," etc. "Shoot! shoot!! shoot!!!" she exclaimed, with a double barrelled pistol in one hand and a long dirk knife in the other, utterly unterrified and fully ready for a death struggle. The male *leader* of the fugitives by this time had "pulled back the hammers" of his "pistols," and was about to fire! Their adversaries seeing the weapons, and the unflinching determination on the part of the *runaways* to stand their ground, "spill blood, kill, or die," rather than be "taken," very prudently "sidled over to the other side of the road," leaving at least four of the victims to travel on their way.

At this moment the four in the carriage lost sight of the two on horseback. Soon after the separation they heard firing, but what the result was, they knew not. They were fearful, however, that their companions had been captured.

The following paragraph, which was shortly afterwards taken from a Southern paper, leaves no room to doubt, as to the fate of the two.

> Six fugitive slaves from Virginia were arrested at the Maryland line, near Hood's Mill, on Christmas day, but, after a severe fight, four of them escaped and have not since been heard of. They came from Loudoun and Fauquier counties.

Though the four who were successful, saw no "severe fight," it is not unreasonable to suppose, that there was a fight, nevertheless; but not till after the number of the fugitives had been reduced to two, instead of six. As chivalrous as slave-holders and slave-catchers were, they knew the value of their precious lives and the fearful risk of attempting a capture, when the numbers were equal.

The party in the carriage, after the conflict, went on their way rejoicing.

The young men, one cold night, when they were compelled to take rest in the woods and snow, in vain strove to keep the feet of their female companions from freezing by lying on them; but the frost was merciless and bit them severely, as their feet very plainly showed. The following disjointed report was cut from the *Frederick (Md.) Examiner*, soon after the occurrence took place:

"Six slaves, four men and two women, fugitives from Virginia, having with them two spring wagons and four horses, came to Hood's Mill, on the Baltimore and Ohio Railroad, near the dividing line between Frederick and Carrol counties, on Christmas day. After feeding their animals, one of them told a Mr. Dixon whence they came; believing them to be fugitives, he spread the alarm, and some eight or ten persons gathered round to arrest them; but the negroes drawing revolvers and bowie-knives, kept their assailants at bay, until five of the party succeeded in escaping in one of the wagons, and as the last one jumped on a horse to flee, he was fired at, the load taking effect in the small of the back. The prisoner says he belongs to Charles W. Simpson, Esq., of Fauquier county, Va., and ran away with the others on the preceding evening."

This report from the *Examiner*, while it is not wholly correct, evidently relates to the fugitives above described. Why the reporter made such glaring mistakes, may be accounted for on the ground that the bold stand made by the fugitives was so bewildering and alarming, that the "assailants" were not in a proper condition to make correct statements. Nevertheless the *Examiner*'s report was preserved with other records, and is here given for what it is worth.

These victims were individually noted on the Record thus: Barnaby was owned by William Rogers, a farmer, who was considered a "moderate slave-holder," although of late "addicted to intemperance." He was the owner of about one "dozen head of slaves," and had besides a wife and two children.

Barnaby's chances for making extra "change" for himself were never favorable; sometimes of "nights" he would manage to earn a "trifle." He was prompted to escape because he "wanted to live by the sweat of his own brow," believing that all men ought so to live. This was the only reason he gave for fleeing.

Mary Elizabeth had been owned by Townsend McVee (likewise a farmer), and in Mary's judgment, he was "severe," but she added, "his wife made him so." McVee owned about twenty-five slaves; "he hardly allowed them to talk—would not allow them to raise chickens," and "only allowed Mary three dresses a year"; the rest she had to get as she could. Sometimes McVee would sell slaves—last year he sold two. Mary said that she could not say anything good of her mistress. On the contrary, she declared that her mistress "knew no mercy nor showed any favor."

It was on account of this "domineering spirit," that Mary was induced to escape.

Frank was owned by Luther Sullivan, "the meanest man in Virginia," he said; he treated his people just as bad as he could in every respect. "Sullivan," added Frank, "would 'lowance the slaves and stint them to save food and get rich," and "would sell and whip," etc. To Frank's knowledge, he had sold some twenty-five head. "He sold my mother and her two children to Georgia some four years previous." But the motive which hurried Frank to make his flight was his laboring under the apprehension that his master had some "pretty heavy creditors who might come on him at any time." Frank, therefore, wanted to be from home in Canada when these gentry should make their visit. My poor mother has been often flogged by master, said Frank. As to his mistress, he said she was "tolerably good."

Ann Wood was owned by McVee also, and was own sister to Elizabeth. Ann very fully sustained her sister Elizabeth's statement respecting the character of her master.

The above-mentioned four, were all young and likely. Barnaby was twenty-six years of age, mulatto, medium size, and intelligent—his wife was about twenty-four years of age, quite dark, good-looking, and of pleasant appearance. Frank was twenty-five years of age, mulatto, and very smart; Ann was twenty-two, good-looking, and smart. After their pressing wants had been met by the Vigilance Committee, and after partial recuperation from their hard travel, etc., they were forwarded on to the Vigilance Committee in New York. In Syracuse, Frank (the leader), who was engaged to Emily, concluded that the knot might as well be tied on the U. G. R. R., although penniless, as to delay the matter a single day longer. Doubtless, the bravery, struggles, and trials of Emily throughout the journey, had, in his estimation, added not a little to her charms. Thus after consulting with her on the matter, her approval was soon obtained, she being too prudent and wise to refuse the hand of one who had proved himself so true a friend to Freedom, as well as so devoted to her. The twain were accordingly made one at the U. G. R. R. Station, in Syracuse, by Superintendent—Rev. J. W. Loguen. After this joyful event, they proceeded to Toronto, and were there gladly received by the Ladies' Society for aiding colored refugees.

The following letter from Mrs. Agnes Willis, wife of the distinguished Rev. Dr. Willis, brought the gratifying intelligence that these brave young adventurers, fell into the hands of distinguished characters and warm friends of Freedom:

TORONTO, 28th January, Monday evening, 1856.

MR. STILL, DEAR SIR:—I have very great pleasure in making you aware that the following respectable persons have arrived here in safety without being annoyed in any way after you saw them. The women, two of them, viz: Mrs. Greegsby and Mrs. Graham, have been rather ailing, but we hope they will very soon be well. They have been attended to by the Ladies' Society, and are most grateful for any attention they have received. The solitary person, Mrs. Graves, has also been attended to; also her box will be looked after. She is pretty well, but rather dull; however, she will get friends and feel more at home by and bye. Mrs. Wanzer is quite well; and also young William Henry Sanderson. They are all of them in pretty good spirits, and I have no doubt they will succeed in whatever business they take up. In the mean time the men are chopping wood, and the ladies are getting plenty sewing. We are always glad to see our colored refugees safe here. I remain, dear sir, yours respectfully,

AGNES WILLIS,
Treasurer to the Ladies' Society to aid colored refugees.

For a time Frank enjoyed his newly won freedom and happy bride with bright prospects all around; but the thought of having left sisters and other relatives in bondage was a source of sadness in the midst of his joy. He was not long, however, in making up his mind that he would deliver them or "die in the attempt." Deliberately forming his plans to go South, he resolved to take upon himself the entire responsibility of all the risks to be encountered. Not a word did he reveal to a living soul of what he was about to undertake. With "twenty-two dollars" in cash and "three pistols" in his pockets, he started in the lightning train from Toronto for Virginia. On reaching Columbia in this State, he deemed it not safe to go any further by public conveyance, consequently he commenced his long journey on foot, and as he neared the slave territory he traveled by night altogether. For two weeks, night and day, he avoided trusting himself in any house, consequently was compelled to lodge in the woods. Nevertheless, during that space of time he succeeded in delivering one of his sisters and her husband, and another friend in the bargain. You can scarcely imagine the Committee's amazement on his return, as they looked upon him and listened to his "noble deeds of daring" and his triumph. A more brave and self-possessed man they had never seen.

He knew what Slavery was and the dangers surrounding him on his mission, but possessing true courage unlike most men, he pictured no alarming difficulties in a distance of nearly one thousand miles by the mail route, through the enemy's country, where he might have in truth said, "I could not pass without running the gauntlet of mobs and assassins, prisons and penitentiaries, bailiffs and constables, &c." If this hero had dwelt upon and magnified the obstacles in his way he would most assuredly have kept off the enemy's country, and his sister and friends would have remained in chains.

The following were the persons delivered by Frank Wanzer. They were his trophies, and this noble act of Frank's should ever be held as a memorial and honor. The Committee's brief record made on their arrival runs thus:

"August 18, 1856. Frank Wanzer, Robert Stewart, alias Gasberry Robison, Vincent Smith, alias John Jackson, Betsey Smith, wife of Vincent Smith, alias Fanny Jackson. They all came from Alder, Loudon county, Virginia."

Robert is about thirty years of age, medium size, dark chestnut color, intelligent and resolute. He was held by the widow Hutchinson, who was also the owner of about one hundred others. Robert regarded her as a "very hard mistress" until the death of her husband, which took place the Fall previous to his escape. That sad affliction, he thought, was the cause of a considerable change in her treatment of her slaves. But yet "nothing was said about freedom," on her part. This reticence Robert understood to mean, that she was still unconverted on this great cardinal principle at least. As he could see no prospect of freedom through her agency, when Frank approached him with a good report from Canada and his friends there, he could scarcely wait to listen to the glorious news; he was so willing and anxious to get out of slavery. His dear old mother, Sarah Davis, and four brothers and two sisters, William, Thomas, Frederick and Samuel, Violet and Ellen, were all owned by Mrs. Hutchinson. Dear as they were to him, he saw no way to take them with him, nor was he prepared to remain a day longer under the yoke; so he decided to accompany Frank, let the cost be what it might.

Vincent is about twenty-three years of age, very "likely-looking," dark color, and more than ordinarily intelligent for one having only the common chances of slaves.

He was owned by the estate of Nathan Skinner, who was "looked upon," by those who knew him, "as a good slave-holder." In slave property, however, he was only interested to the number of twelve head. Skinner "neither sold nor emancipated." A year and a half before Vincent escaped, his master was called to give an account of his stewardship, and there in the spirit land Vincent was willing to let him remain, without much more to add about him.

Vincent left his mother, Judah Smith, and brothers and sisters, Edwin, Angeline, Sina Ann, Adaline Susan, George, John and Lewis, all belonging to the estate of Skinner.

Vincent was fortunate enough to bring his wife along with him. She was about twenty-seven years of age, of a brown color, and smart, and was owned by the daughter of the widow Hutchinson. This mistress was said to be a "clever woman."

"Sam," "Isaac," "Perry," "Charles," and "Green"

ONE THOUSAND DOLLARS REWARD.—Ran away on Saturday night, the 20th September, 1856, from the subscriber, living in the ninth district of Carroll county, Maryland, two Negro Men, SAM and ISAAC. Sam calls himself Samuel Sims; he is very black; shows his teeth very much when he laughs; no perceptible marks; he is 5 feet 8 inches high, and about thirty years of age, but has the appearance of being much older.

Isaac calls himself Isaac Dotson he is about nineteen years of age, stout made, but rather chunky; broad across his shoulders, he is about five feet five or six inches high, always appears to be in a good humor; laughs a good deal, and runs on with a good deal of foolishness; he is of very light color, almost yellow, might be called a yellow boy; has no perceptible marks.

They have such a variety of clothing that it is almost useless to say anything about them. No doubt they will change their names.

I will give the above reward for them, of one thousand dollars, or five hundred dollars for either of them, if taken and lodged in any jail in Maryland so that I get them again.

Also two of Mr. Dade's, living in the neighborhood, went the same time; no doubt they are all in company together.

s24—6tWit* THOMAS B. OWINGS.

☞ These passengers reached the Philadelphia station, about the 24th of September, 1856, five days after they escaped from Carroll county. They were in fine spirits, and had borne the fatigue and privation of travel bravely. A free and interesting interview took place, between these passengers and the Committee, eliciting much information, especially with regard to the workings of the system on the farms, from which they had the good luck to flee. Each of the party was thoroughly questioned, about how time had passed with them at home, or rather in the prison house, what kind of men their masters were, how they fed and clothed, if they whipped, bought or sold, whether they were members of church, or not, and many more questions needless to enumerate bearing on the domestic relation which had existed between themselves and their masters. These queries they answered in their own way, with intelligence. Upon the whole, their lot in Slavery had been rather more favorable than the average run of slaves.

No record was made of any very severe treatment. In fact, the notices made of them were very brief, and, but for the elaborate way in which they were described in the "Baltimore Sun," by their owners, their narratives would hardly be considered of sufficient interest to record. The heavy rewards, beautiful descriptions, and elegant illustrations in the "Sun," were very attractive reading. The Vigilance Committee took the "Sun," for nothing else under the sun but for this special literature, and for this purpose they always considered the "Sun" a cheap and reliable paper.

A slave man or woman, running for life, he with a bundle on his back or she with a babe in her arms, was always a very interesting sight, and should always be held in remembrance. Likewise the descriptions given by slave-holders, as a general rule, showed considerable artistic powers and a most thorough knowledge of the physical outlines of this peculiar property. Indeed, the art must have been studied attentively for practical purposes. When the advertisements were received in advance of arrivals, which was always the case, the descriptions generally were found so lifelike, that the Committee preferred to take them in preference to putting themselves to the labor of writing out new ones, for future reference. This we think, ought not to be complained of by any who were so unfortunate as to lose wayward servants, as it is but fair to give credit to all concerned. True, sometimes some of these beautiful advertisements were open to gentle criticism. The one at the head of this report, is clearly of this character. For instance, in describing Isaac, Mr. Thomas B. Owings, represents him as being of a "very light color," "almost yellow," "might be called a yellow boy." In the next breath he has no perceptible marks. Now, if he is "very light," that is a well-known southern mark, admitted everywhere. A hint to the wise is sufficient. However, judging from what was seen of Isaac in Philadelphia, there was more cunning than "foolishness" about him. Slaves sometimes, when wanting to get away, would make their owners believe that they were very happy and contented. And, in using this kind of foolishness, would keep up appearances until an opportunity offered for an escape. So Isaac might have possessed this sagacity, which appeared like nonsense to his master. That slave-holders, above all others, were in the habit of taking special pains to encourage foolishness, loud laughing, banjo playing, low dancing, etc., in the place of education, virtue, self-respect and manly carriage, slave-holders themselves are witnesses.

As Mr. Robert Dade was also a loser, equally with Mr. Thomas B. Owings, and as his advertisement was of the same liberality and high tone, it seems but fitting that it should come in just here, to give weight and completeness to the story. Both Owings and Dade showed a considerable degree of southern chivalry in the liberality of their rewards. Doubtless, the large sums thus offered awakened a lively feeling in the breasts of old slave-hunters. But it is to be supposed that the artful fugitives safely reached Philadelphia before the hunters got even the first scent on their track. Up to the present hour, with the owners all may be profound mystery; if so, it is to be hoped, that they may feel some interest in the solution of these wonders. The articles so accurately described must now be permitted to testify in their own words, as taken from the records.

GREEN MODOCK acknowledges that he was owned by William Dorsey, Perry by Robert Dade, Sam and Isaac by Thomas Owings, all farmers, and all "tough" and "pretty mean men." Sam and Isaac had other names with them, but not such a variety of clothing as their master might have supposed. Sam said he left because his master threatened to sell him to Georgia, and he believed that he meant so to do, as he had sold all his brothers and sisters to Georgia some time before he escaped.

But this was not all. Sam declared his master had threatened to shoot him a short while before he left. This was the last straw on the camel's back. Sam's heart was in Canada ever after that. In traveling he resolved that nothing should stop him. Charles offered the same excuse as did Sam. He had been threatened with the auction-block. He left his mother free, but four sisters he left in chains. As these men spoke of their tough owners and bad treatment in Slavery, they expressed their indignation at the idea that Owings, Dade and Dorsey had dared to rob them of their God-given rights. They were only ignorant farm hands. As they drank in the free air, the thought of their wrongs aroused all their manhood. They were all young men, hale and stout, with strong resolutions to make Canada their future home. The Committee encouraged them in this, and aided them for humanity's sake.—Mr. Robert Dade's advertisement speaks for itself as follows:

RAN AWAY—On Saturday night, 20th inst., from the subscriber, living near Mount Airy P. O., Carroll county, two Negro men, PERRY and CHARLES. Perry is quite dark, full face; is about 5 feet 8 or 9 inches high; has a scar on one of his hands, and one on his legs, caused by a cut from a scythe; 25 years old. Charles is of a copper color, about 5 feet 9 or 10 inches high; round shouldered, with small whiskers; has one crooked finger that he cannot straighten, and a scar on his right leg, caused by the cut of a scythe; 22 years old. I will give two hundred and fifty dollars each, if taken in the State and returned to me, or secured in some jail so that I can get them again, or a $1,000 for the two, or $500 each, if taken out of the State, and secured in some jail in this State so that I can get them again.

s23—3f.   ROBERT DADE.

Escaping in a Chest

$150 REWARD. Ran away from the subscriber, on Sunday night, 27th inst., my NEGRO GIRL, Lear Green, about 18 years of age, black complexion, round-featured, good-looking and ordinary size; she had on and with her when she left, a tan-colored silk bonnet, a dark plaid silk dress, a light mouslin delaine, also one watered silk cape and one tan colored cape. I have reason to be confident that she was persuaded off by a negro man named Wm. Adams, black, quick spoken, 5 feet 10 inches high, a large scar on one side of his face, running down in a ridge by the corner of his mouth, about 4 inches long, barber by trade, but works mostly about taverns, opening oysters, &c. He has been missing about a week; he had been heard to say he was going to marry the above girl and ship to New York, where it is said his mother resides. The above reward will be paid if said girl is taken out of the State of Maryland and delivered to me; or fifty dollars if taken in the State of Maryland.

M26-3T

JAMES NOBLE,
No. 153, Broadway, Baltimore.

Lear Green, so particularly advertised in the "Baltimore Sun" by "James Noble," won for herself a strong claim to a high place among the heroic women of the nineteenth century. In regard to description and age the advertisement is tolerably accurate, although her master might have added, that her countenance was one of peculiar modesty and grace. Instead of being "black," she was of a "dark-brown color." Of her bondage she made the following statement: She was owned by "James Noble, a Butter Dealer" of Baltimore. He fell heir to Lear by the will of his wife's mother, Mrs. Rachel Howard, by whom she had previously been owned. Lear was but a mere child when she came into the hands of Noble's family. She, therefore, remembered but little of her old mistress. Her young mistress, however, had made a lasting impression upon her mind; for she was very exacting and oppressive in regard to the tasks she was daily in the habit of laying upon Lear's shoulders, with no disposition whatever to allow her any liberties. At least Lear was never indulged in this respect. In this situation a young man by the name of William Adams proposed marriage to her. This offer she was inclined to accept, but disliked the idea of being encumbered with the chains of slavery and the duties of a family at the same time.

After a full consultation with her mother and also her intended upon the matter, she decided that she must be free in order to fill the station of a wife and mother. For a time dangers and difficulties in the way of escape seemed utterly to set at defiance all hope of success. Whilst every pulse was beating strong for liberty, only one chance seemed to be left, the trial of which required as much courage as it would to endure the cutting off the right arm or plucking out the right eye. An old chest of substantial make, such as sailors commonly use, was procured. A quilt, a pillow, and a few articles of raiment, with a small quantity of food and a bottle of water were put in it, and Lear placed therein; strong ropes were fastened around the chest and she was safely stowed amongst the ordinary freight on one of the Erricson line of steamers. Her intended's mother, who was a free woman, agreed to come as a passenger on the same boat. How could she refuse? The prescribed rules of the Company assigned colored passengers to the deck. In this instance it was exactly where this guardian and mother desired to be—as near the chest as possible. Once or twice, during the silent watches of the night, she was drawn irresistibly to the chest, and could not refrain from venturing to untie the rope and raise the lid a little, to see if the poor child still lived, and at the same time to give her a breath of fresh air. Without uttering a whisper, that frightful moment, this office was successfully performed. That the silent prayers of this oppressed young woman, together with her faithful protector's, were momentarily ascending to the ear of the good God above, there can be no question. Nor is it to be doubted for a moment but that some ministering angel aided the mother to unfasten the rope, and at the same time nerved the heart of poor Lear to endure the trying ordeal of her perilous situation. She declared that she had no fear.

After she had passed eighteen hours in the chest, the steamer arrived at the wharf in Philadelphia, and in due time the living freight was brought off the boat, and at first was delivered at a house in Barley street, occupied by particular friends of the mother. Subsequently chest and freight were removed to the residence of the writer, in whose family she remained several days under the protection and care of the Vigilance Committee.

Such hungering and thirsting for liberty, as was evinced by Lear Green, made the efforts of the most ardent friends, who were in the habit of aiding fugitives, seem feeble in the extreme. Of all the heroes in Canada, or out of it, who have purchased their liberty by downright bravery, through perils the most hazardous, none deserve more praise than Lear Green.

She remained for a time in this family, and was then forwarded to Elmira. In this place she was married to William Adams, who has been previously alluded to. They never went to Canada, but took up their permanent abode in Elmira. The brief space of about three years only was allotted her in which to enjoy freedom, as death came and terminated her career. About the time of this sad occurrence, her mother-in-law died in this city. The impressions made by both mother and daughter can never be effaced. The chest in which Lear escaped has been preserved by the writer as a rare trophy, and her photograph taken, while in the chest, is an excellent likeness of her and, at the same time, a fitting memorial.

The Slave-hunting Tragedy in Lancaster County, in September, 1851

"TREASON AT CHRISTIANA"

⌘ Having inserted the Fugitive Slave Bill in these records of the Underground Rail Road, one or two slave cases will doubtless suffice to illustrate the effect of its passage on the public mind, and the colored people in particular. The deepest feelings of loathing, contempt and opposition were manifested by the opponents of Slavery on every hand. Anti-slavery papers, lecturers, preachers, etc., arrayed themselves boldly against it on the ground of its inhumanity and violation of the laws of God.

On the other hand, the slave-holders South, and their pro-slavery adherents in the North demanded the most abject obedience from all parties, regardless of conscience or obligation to God. In order to compel such obedience, as well as to prove the practicability of the law, unbounded zeal daily marked the attempt on the part of slaveholders and slave-catchers to refasten the fetters on the limbs of fugitives in different parts of the North, whither they had escaped.

In this dark hour, when colored men's rights were so insecure, as a matter of self-defence, they felt called upon to arm themselves and resist all kidnapping intruders, although clothed with the authority of wicked law. Among the most exciting cases tending to justify this course, the following may be named:

JAMES HAMLET was the first slave case who was summarily arrested under the Fugitive Slave Law, and sent back to bondage from New York.

WILLIAM AND ELLEN CRAFT were hotly pursued to Boston by hunters from Georgia.

ADAM GIBSON, a free colored man, residing in Philadelphia, was arrested, delivered into the hands of his alleged claimants, by commissioner Edward D. Ingraham, and hurried into Slavery.

EUPHEMIA WILLIAMS (the mother of six living children),—her case excited much interest and sympathy.

SHADRACH was arrested and rescued in Boston.

HANNAH DELLUM and her child were returned to Slavery from Philadelphia.

THOMAS HALL and his wife were pounced upon at midnight in Chester county, beaten and dragged off to Slavery, etc.

And, as if gloating over their repeated successes, and utterly regardless of all caution, about one year after the passage of this nefarious bill, a party of slave-hunters arranged for a grand capture at Christiana.

One year from the passage of the law, at a time when alarm and excitement were running high, the most decided stand was taken at Christiana, in the State of Pennsylvania, to defeat the law, and defend freedom. Fortunately for the fugitives the plans of the slave-hunters and officials leaked out while arrangements were making in Philadelphia for the capture, and, information being sent to the Anti-slavery office, a messenger was at once dispatched to Christiana to put all persons supposed to be in danger on their guard.

Among those thus notified, were brave hearts, who did not believe in running away from slave-catchers. They resolved to stand up for the right of self-defence. They loved liberty and hated Slavery, and when the slave-catchers arrived, they were prepared for them. Of the contest, on that bloody morning, we have copied a report, carefully written at the time, by C. M. Burleigh, editor of the "Pennsylvania Freeman," who visited the scene of battle, immediately after it was over, and doubtless obtained as faithful an account of all the facts in the case, as could then be had.

"Last Thursday morning, (the 11th inst.), a peaceful neighborhood in the borders of Lancaster county, was made the scene of a bloody battle, resulting from an attempt to capture seven colored men as fugitive slaves. As the reports of the affray which came to us were contradictory, and having good reason to believe that those of the daily press were grossly one-sided and unfair, we repaired to the scene of the tragedy, and, by patient inquiry and careful examination, endeavered to learn the real facts. To do this, from the varying and conflicting statements which we encountered, scarcely two of which agreed in every point, was not easy; but we believe the account we give below, as the result of these inquiries, is substantially correct.

Very early on the 11th inst. a party of slave-hunters went into a neighborhood about two miles west of Christiana, near the eastern border of Lancaster county, in pursuit of fugitive slaves. The party consisted of Edward Gorsuch, his son, Dickerson Gorsuch, his nephew, Dr. Pearce, Nicholas Hutchins, and others, all from Baltimore county, Md., and one Henry H. Kline, a notorious slave-catching constable from Philadelphia, who had been deputized by Commissioner Ingraham for this business. At about day-dawn they were discovered lying in an ambush near the house of one William Parker, a colored man, by an inmate of the house, who had started for his work. He fled back to the house, pursued by the slave-hunters, who entered the lower part of the house, but were unable to force their way into the upper part, to which the family had retired. A horn was blown from an upper window; two shots were fired, both, as we believe, though we are not certain, by the assailants, one at the colored man who fled into the house, and the other at the inmates, through the window. No one was wounded by either. A parley ensued. The slave-holder demanded his slaves, who he said were concealed in the house. The colored men presented themselves successively at the window, and asked if they were the slaves claimed; Gorsuch said, that neither of them was his slave. They told him that they were the only colored men in the house, and were determined never to be taken alive as slaves. Soon the colored people of the neighborhood, alarmed by the horn, began to gather, armed with guns, axes, corn-cutters, or clubs. Mutual threatenings were uttered by the two parties. The slave-holders told the blacks that resistance would be useless, as they had a party of thirty men in the woods near by. The blacks warned them again to leave, as they would die before they would go into Slavery.

From an hour to an hour and a half passed in these parleyings, angry conversations, and threats; the blacks increasing by new arrivals, until they probably numbered from thirty to fifty, most of them armed in some way. About this time, Castner Hanaway, a white man, and a Friend, who resided in the neighborhood, rode up, and was soon followed by Elijah Lewis, another Friend, a merchant, in Cooperville, both gentlemen highly esteemed as worthy and peaceable citizens. As they came up, Kline, the deputy marshal, ordered them to aid him, as a United States officer, to capture the fugitive slaves. They refused of course, as would any man not utterly destitute of honor, humanity, and moral principle, and warned the assailants that it was madness for them to attempt to capture fugitive slaves there, or even to remain, and begged them if they wished to save their own lives, to leave the ground. Kline replied, "Do you really think so?" "Yes," was the answer, "the sooner you leave, the better, if you would prevent bloodshed." Kline then left the ground, retiring into a very safe distance into a cornfield, and toward the woods. The blacks were so exasperated by his threats, that, but for the interposition of the two white Friends, it is very doubtful whether he would have escaped without injury. Messrs. Hanaway and Lewis both exerted their influence to dissuade the colored people from violence, and would probably have succeeded in restraining them, had not the assailing party fired upon them. Young Gorsuch asked his father to leave, but the old man refused, declaring, as it is said and believed, that he would "go to hell, or have his slaves."

Finding they could do nothing further, Hanaway and Lewis both started to leave, again counselling the slave-hunters to go away, and the colored people to peace, but had gone but a few rods, when one of the inmates of the house attempted to come out at the door. Gorsuch presented his revolver, ordering him back. The colored man replied, "You had better go away, if you don't want to get hurt," and at the same time pushed him aside and passed out. Maddened at this, and stimulated by the question of his nephew, whether he would "take such an insult from a d—d nigger," Gorsuch fired at the colored man,

The Christiana tragedy.

and was followed by his son and nephew, who both fired their revolvers. The fire was returned by the blacks, who made a rush upon
them at the same time. Gorsuch and his son fell, the one dead the
other wounded. The rest of the party after firing their revolvers, fled
precipitately through the corn and to the woods, pursued by some of
the blacks. One was wounded, the rest escaped unhurt. Kline, the
deputy marshal, who now boasts of his miraculous escape from a volley of musketballs, had kept at a safe distance, though urged by young
Gorsuch to stand by his father and protect him, when he refused to
leave the ground. He of course came off unscathed. Several colored
men were wounded, but none severely. Some had their hats or their
clothes perforated with bullets; others had flesh wounds. They said
that the Lord protected them, and they shook the bullets from their
clothes. One man found several shot in his boot, which seemed to
have spent their force before reaching him, and did not even break the
skin. The slave-holders having fled, several neighbors, mostly Friends
and anti-slavery men, gathered to succor the wounded and take
charge of the dead. We are told that Parker himself protected the
wounded man from his excited comrades, and brought water and a

bed from his own house for the invalid, thus showing that he was as magnanimous to his fallen enemy as he was brave in the defence of his own liberty. The young man was then removed to a neighboring house, where the family received him with the tenderest kindness and paid him every attention, though they told him in Quaker phrase, that "they had no unity with his cruel business," and were very sorry to see him engaged in it. He was much affected by their kindness, and we are told, expressed his regret that he had been thus engaged, and his determination, if his life was spared, never again to make a similar attempt. His wounds are very severe, and it is feared mortal. All attempts to procure assistance to capture the fugitive slaves failed, the people in the neighborhood either not relishing the business of slave-catching, or at least, not choosing to risk their lives in it. There was a very great reluctance felt to going even to remove the body and the wounded man, until several abolitionists and Friends had collected for that object, when others found courage to follow on. The excitement caused by this most melancholy affair is very great among all classes. The abolitionists, of course, mourn the occurrence, while they see in it a legitimate fruit of the Fugitive Slave Law, just such a harvest of blood as they had long feared that the law would produce, and which they had earnestly labored to prevent. We believe that they alone, of all classes of the nation, are free from responsibility for its occurrence, having wisely foreseen the danger, and faithfully labored to avert it by removing its causes, and preventing the inhuman policy which has hurried on the bloody convulsion.

The enemies of the colored people, are making this the occasion of fresh injuries, and a more bitter ferocity toward that defenceless people, and of new misrepresentation and calumnies against the abolitionists.

The colored people, though the great body of them had no connection with this affair, are hunted like partridges upon the mountains, by the relentless horde which has been poured forth upon them, under the pretense of arresting the parties concerned in the fight. When we reached Christiana, on Friday afternoon, we found that the Deputy-Attorney Thompson, of Lancaster, was there, and had issued warrants, upon the depositions of Kline and others, for the arrest of all suspected persons. A company of police were scouring the neighborhood in search of colored people, several of whom were seized while at their work near by, and brought in.

CASTNER HANAWAY and Elijah Lewis, hearing that warrants were issued against them, came to Christiana, and voluntarily gave themselves up, calm and strong in the confidence of their innocence. They, together with the arrested colored men, were sent to Lancaster jail that night.

The next morning we visited the ground of the battle, and the family where young Gorsuch now lives, and while there, we saw a deposition which he had just made, that he believed no white persons were engaged in the affray, beside his own party. As he was on the ground during the whole controversy, and deputy Marshall Kline had discreetly run off into the corn-field, before the fighting began, the hireling slave-catcher's eager and confident testimony against our white friends, will, we think, weigh lightly with impartial men.

On returning to Christiana, we found that the United States Marshal from the city, had arrived at that place, accompanied by Commissioner Ingraham, Mr. Jones, a special commissioner of the United States, from Washington, the U. S. District Attorney Ashmead, with forty-five U. S. Marines from the Navy Yard, and a posse of about forty of the City Marshal's police, together with a large body of special constables, eager for such a manhunt, from Columbia and Lancaster and other places. This crowd divided into parties, of from ten to twenty-five, and scoured the country, in every direction, for miles around, ransacking the houses of the colored people, and captured every colored man they could find, with several colored women, and two other white men. Never did our heart bleed with deeper pity for the peeled and persecuted colored people, than when we saw this troop let loose upon them, and witnessed the terror and distress which its approach excited in families, wholly innocent of the charges laid against them."

On the other hand, a few extracts from the editorials of some of the leading papers, will suffice to show the state of public feeling at that time, and the dreadful opposition abolitionists and fugitives had to contend with.

From one of the leading daily journals of Philadelphia, we copy as follows:

"There can be no difference of opinion concerning the shocking affair which occurred at Christiana, on Thursday, the resisting of a law of Congress by a band of armed negroes, whereby the majesty of the Government was defied and life taken in one and the same act. There is something more than a mere ordinary, something more than even a murderous, riot in all this. It is an act of insurrection, we might, considering the peculiar class and condition of the guilty parties, almost call it a servile insurrection—if not also one of treason. Fifty, eighty, or a hundred persons, whether white or black, who are deliberately in arms for the purpose of resisting the law, even the law for the recovery of fugitive slaves, are in the attitude of levying war against the United States; and doubly heavy becomes the crime of murder in such a case, and doubly serious the accountability of all who have any connection with the act as advisers, suggesters, countenancers, or accessories in any way whatever."

In those days, the paper from which this extract is taken, represented the Whig party and the more moderate and respectable class of citizens.

The following is an extract from a leading democratic organ of Philadelphia:

"We will not, however, insult the reader by arguing that which has not been heretofore doubted, and which is not doubted now, by ten honest men in the State, and that is that the abolitionists are implicated in the Christiana murder. All the ascertained facts go to show that they were the real, if not the chief instigators. White men are known to harbor fugitives, in the neighborhood of Christiana, and these white men are known to be abolitionists, known to be opposed to the Fugitive Slave Law, and *known* to be the warm friends of William F. Johnston, (Governor of the State of Pennsylvania). And, as if to clinch the argument, no less than three white men are now in the Lancaster prison, and were arrested as accomplices in the dreadful affair on the morning of the eleventh. And one of these white men was committed on a charge of high treason, on Saturday last, by United States Commissioner Ingraham."

Another daily paper of opposite politics thus spake:

"The unwarrantable outrage committed last week, at Christiana, Lancaster county, is a foul stain upon the fair name and fame of our State. We are pleased to see that the officers of the Federal and State Governments are upon the tracks of those who were engaged in the riot, and that several arrests have been made.

We do not wish to see the poor misled blacks who participated in the affair, suffer to any great extent, for they were but tools. The men who are really chargeable with treason against the United States Government, and with the death of Mr. Gorsuch, an estimable citizen of Maryland, are unquestionably *white*, with hearts black enough to incite them to the commission of any crime equal in atrocity to that committed in Lancaster county. Pennsylvania has now but one course to pursue, and that is to aid, and warmly aid, the United States in bringing to condign punishment, every man engaged in the riot. She owes it to herself and to the Union. Let her in this resolve, be just and fearless."

From a leading neutral daily paper the following is taken: "One would suppose from the advice of forcible resistance, so familiarly given by the abolitionists, that they are quite unaware that there is any such crime as treason recognized by the Constitution, or punished with death by the laws of the United States. We would remind them, that not only is there such a crime, but that there is a solemn decision of the Supreme Court, that all who are concerned in a conspiracy which ripens into treason, whether present or absent from the scene of actual violence, are involved in the same liabilities as the immediate actors. If they engage in the conspiracy and stimulate the treason, they may keep their bodies from the affray without saving their necks from a halter.

It would be very much to the advantage of society, if an example could be made of some of these persistent agitators, who excite the ignorant and reckless to treasonable violence, from which they themselves shrink, but who are, not only in morals, but in law, equally guilty and equally amenable to punishment with the victims of their inflammatory counsels."

A number of the most influential citizens represented the occurrence to the Governor as follows:

"To the Governor of Pennsylvania:

The undersigned, citizens of Pennsylvania, respectfully represent:

That citizens of a neighboring State have been cruelly assassinated by a band of armed outlaws at a place not more than three hours' journey distant from the seat of Government and from the commercial metropolis of this State:

That this insurrectionary movement in one of the most populous parts of the State has been so far successful as to overawe the local ministers of justice and paralyze the power of the law:

That your memorialists are not aware that 'any military force' has been sent to the seat of insurrection, or that the civil authority has been strengthened by the adoption of any measures suited to the momentous crisis.

They, therefore, respectfully request the chief executive magistrate of Pennsylvania to take into consideration the necessity of vindicating the outraged laws, and sustaining the dignity of the Commonwealth on this important and melancholy occasion."

Under this high pressure of public excitement, threatening and alarm breathed so freely on every hand, that fugitive slaves and their friends in this region of Pennsylvania at least, were compelled to pass through an hour of dreadful darkness—an ordeal extremely trying. The authorities of the United States, as well as the authorities of the State of Pennsylvania and Maryland, were diligently making arrests wherever a suspected party could be found, who happened to belong in the neighborhood of Christiana.

In a very short time the following persons were in custody: J. Castner Hanaway, Elijah Lewis, Joseph Scarlett, Samuel Kendig, Henry Spins, George Williams, Charles Hunter, Wilson Jones, Francis Harkins, Benjamin Thomson, William Brown (No. 1), William Brown (No. 2), John Halliday, Elizabeth Mosey, John Morgan, Joseph Berry, John Norton, Denis Smith, Harvey Scott, Susan Clark,

Tansy Brown, Eliza Brown, Eliza Parker, Hannah Pinckney, Robert Johnson, Miller Thompson, Isaiah Clark, and Jonathan Black.

These were not all, but sufficed for a beginning; at least it made an interesting entertainment for the first day's examination; and although there were two or three non-resistant Quakers, and a number of poor defenceless colored women among those thus taken as prisoners, still it seemed utterly impossible for the exasperated defenders of Slavery to divest themselves of the idea, that this heroic deed, in self-defence, on the part of men who felt that their liberties were in danger, was anything less than actually levying war against the United States.

Accordingly, therefore, the hearing gravely took place at Lancaster. On the side of the Commonwealth, the following distinguished counsel appeared on examination: Hon. John L. Thompson, District Attorney; Wm. B. Faulney, Esq.; Thos. E. Franklin, Esq., Attorney-General of Lancaster county; George L. Ashmead, Esq., of Philadelphia, representative of the United States authorities; and Hon. Robert Brent, Attorney-General of Maryland.

For the defence—Hon. Thaddeus Stevens, Reah Frazer, Messrs. Ford, Cline, and Dickey, Esquires.

From a report of the first day's hearing we copy a short extract, as follows:

"The excitement at Christiana, during yesterday, was very great. Several hundred persons were present, and the deepest feeling was manifested against the perpetrators of the outrage. At two o'clock yesterday afternoon, the United States Marshal, Mr. Roberts, United States District Attorney, J. H. Ashmead, Esq., Mr. Commissioner Ingraham, and Recorder Lee, accompanied by the United States Marines, returned to the city. Lieut. Johnson, and officers Lewis S. Brest, Samuel Mitchell, Charles McCully, Samuel Neff, Jacob Albright, Robert McEwen, and—Perkenpine, by direction of the United States Marshal, had charge of the following named prisoners, who were safely lodged in Moyamensing prison, accompanied by the Marines:—Joseph Scarlett, (white), William Brown, Ezekiel Thompson, Isaiah Clarkson, Daniel Caulsberry, Benjamin Pendergrass, Elijah Clark, George W. H. Scott, Miller Thompson, and

Samuel Hanson, all colored. The last three were placed in the debtors' apartment, and the others in the criminal apartment of the Moyamensing prison to await their trial for treason, &c."

In alluding to the second day's doings, the Philadelphia Ledger thus represented matters at the field of battle:

"The intelligence received last evening, represents the country for miles around, to be in as much excitement as at any time since the horrible deed was committed. The officers sent there at the instance of the proper authorities are making diligent search in every direction, and securing every person against whom the least suspicion is attached. The police force from this city, amounting to about sixty men, are under the marshalship of Lieut. Ellis. Just as the cars started east, in the afternoon, five more prisoners who were secured at a place called the Welsh Mountains, twelve miles distant, were brought into Christiana. They were placed in custody until such time as a hearing will take place."

Although the government had summoned its ablest legal talent and the popular sentiment was as a hundred to one against William Parker and his brave comrades who had made the slave-hunter "bite the dust," most nobly did Thaddeus Stevens prove that he was not to be cowed, that he believed in the stirring sentiment so much applauded by the American people, "Give me liberty, or give me death," not only for the white man but for all men. Thus standing upon such great and invulnerable principles, it was soon discovered that one could chase a thousand, and two put ten thousand to flight in latter as well as in former times.

At first even the friends of freedom thought that the killing of Gorsuch was not only wrong, but unfortunate for the cause. Scarcely a week passed, however, before the matter was looked upon in a far different light, and it was pretty generally thought that, if the Lord had not a direct hand in it, the cause of Freedom at least would be greatly benefited thereby.

And just in proportion as the masses cried, Treason! Treason! the hosts of freedom from one end of the land to the other were awakened to sympathize with the slave. Thousands were soon aroused to show sympathy who had hitherto been dormant. Hundreds visited the prisoners in their cells to greet, cheer, and offer them aid and counsel in their hour of sore trial.

The friends of freedom remained calm even while the pro-slavery party were fiercely raging and gloating over the prospect, as they evidently thought of the satisfaction to be derived from teaching the abolitionists a lesson from the scaffold, which would in future prevent Underground Rail Road passengers from killing their masters when in pursuit of them.

Through the efforts of the authorities three white men, and twenty-seven colored had been safely lodged in Moyamensing prison, under the charge of treason. The authorities, however, had utterly failed to catch the hero, William Parker, as he had been sent to Canada, *via* the Underground Rail Road, and was thus "sitting under his own vine and fig tree, where none dared to molest, or make him afraid."

As an act of simple justice it may here be stated that the abolitionists and prisoners found a true friend and ally at least in one United States official, who, by the way, figured prominently in making arrests, etc., namely: the United States Marshal, A. E. Roberts. In all his intercourse with the prisoners and their friends, he plainly showed that all his sympathies were on the side of Freedom, and not with the popular pro-slavery sentiment which clamored so loudly against traitors and abolitionists.

Two of his prisoners had been identified in the jail as fugitive slaves by their owners. When the trial came on these two individuals were among the missing. How they escaped was unknown; the Marshal, however, was strongly suspected of being a friend of the Underground Rail Road, and to add now, that those suspicions were founded on fact, will, doubtless, do him no damage.

In order to draw the contrast between Freedom and Slavery, simply with a view of showing how the powers that were acted and judged in the days of the reign of the Fugitive Slave Law, unquestionably nothing better could be found to meet the requirements of this issue than the charge of Judge Kane, coupled with the indictment of the Grand Jury. In the light of the Emancipation and the Fifteenth Amendment, they are too transparent to need a single word of comment. Judge and jury having found the accused chargeable with Treason, nothing remained, so far as the men were concerned, but to bide their time as best they could in prison. Most of them were married, and had wives and children clinging to them in this hour of fearful looking for judgment.

The Law of Treason, as Laid Down by Judge Kane

⛫ The following charge to the Grand Jury of the United States District Court, in reference to the Slave-hunting affray in Lancaster county, and preparatory to their finding bills of indictment against the prisoners, was delivered on Monday, September 28, by Judge Kane:

"Gentlemen of the Grand Jury:—It has been represented to me, that since we met last, circumstances have occurred in one of the neighboring counties in our District, which should call for your prompt scrutiny, and perhaps for the energetic action of the Court. It is said, that a citizen of the State of Maryland, who had come into Pennsylvania to reclaim a fugitive from labor, was forcibly obstructed in the attempt by a body of armed men, assaulted, beaten and murdered; that some members of his family, who had accompanied him in the pursuit, were at the same time, and by the same party maltreated and grievously wounded; and that an officer of justice, constituted under the authority of this Court, who sought to arrest the fugitive, was impeded and repelled by menaces and violence, while proclaiming his character, and exhibiting his warrant. It is said, too, that the time and manner of these outrages, their asserted object, the denunciations by which they were preceded, and the simultaneous action of most of the guilty parties, evinced a combined purpose forcibly to resist and make nugatory a constitutional provision, and the statutes enacted in pursuance of it: and it is added, in confirmation of this, that for some months back, gatherings of people, strangers, as well as citizens, have been held from time to time in the vicinity of the place of the recent outbreaks, at which exhortations were made and pledges interchanged to hold the law for the recovery of fugitive slaves as of no validity, and to defy its execution. Such are some of the representations that have been made in my hearing, and in regard to which, it has become your duty, as the Grand Inquest of the District, to make legal inquiry. Personally, I know nothing of the facts, or the evidence relating to them. As a member of the Court, before which the accused persons may hereafter be arraigned and tried, I have sought to keep my mind altogether free from any impressions of their guilt or innocence, and even from an extra-judicial knowledge of the circumstances which must determine the legal character of the offence that has thus been perpetrated. It is due to the great interests of public justice, no less than to the parties implicated in a criminal charge, that their cause should be in no wise and in no degree prejudged. And in referring, therefore, to the representations which have been made to me, I have no other object than to point you to the reasons for my addressing you at this advanced period of our sessions, and to enable you to apply with more facility and certainty the principles and rules of law, which I shall proceed to lay before you.

If the circumstances, to which I have adverted, have in fact taken place, they involve the highest crime known to our laws. Treason against the United States is defined by the Constitution, Art. 3, Sec. 3, cl. 1, to consist in "levying war against them, or adhering to their enemies, giving them aid and comfort." This definition is borrowed from the ancient Law of England, Stat. 25, Edw. 3, Stat. 5, Chap. 2, and its terms must be understood, of course, in the sense which they bore in that law, and which obtained here when the Constitution was adopted. The expression, "levying war," so regarded, embraces not merely the act of formal or declared war, but any combination forcibly to prevent or oppose the execution or enforcement of a provision of the Constitution, or of a public Statute, if accompanied or followed by an act of forcible opposition in pursuance of such combination. This, in substance, has been the interpretation given to these words by the English Judges, and it has been uniformly and fully recognized and adopted in the Courts of the United States. (See Foster, Hale, and Hawkins, and the opinions of Iredell, Patterson, Chase, Marshall, and Washington, J. J., of the Supreme Court, and of Peters, D. J., in U. S. vs. Vijol, U. S. vs. Mitchell, U. S. vs. Fries, U. S. vs. Bollman and Swartwout, and U. S. vs. Burr).

The definition, as you will observe, includes two particulars, both of them indispensable elements of the offence. There must have been a combination or conspiring together to oppose the law by force, and some actual force must have been exerted, or the crime of treason is not consummated. The highest, or at least the direct proof of the combination may be found in the declared purposes of the individual party before the actual outbreak; or it may be derived from the proceedings of meetings, in which he took part openly; or which he either prompted, or made effective by his countenance or sanction,—commending, counselling and instigating forcible resistance to the law. I speak, of course, of a conspiring to resist a law, not the more limited purpose to violate it, or to prevent its application and enforcement in a particular case, or against a particular individual. The combination must be directed against the law itself. But such direct proof of this element of the offence is not legally necessary to establish its existence. The concert of purpose may be deduced from the concerted action itself, or it may be inferred from facts occurring at the time, or afterwards, as well as before. Besides this, there must be some act of violence, as the result or consequence of the combining.

But here again, it is not necessary to prove that the individual accused was a direct, personal actor in the violence. If he was present, directing, aiding, abetting, counselling, or countenancing it, he is in law guilty of the forcible act. Nor is even his personal presence indispensable. Though he be absent at the time of its actual perpetration, yet, if he directed the act, devised, or knowingly furnished the means for carrying it into effect, instigated others to perform it, he shares their guilt.

In treason there are no accessories. There has been, I fear, an erroneous impression on this subject, among a portion of our people. If it has been thought safe, to counsel and instigate others to acts of forcible oppugnation to the provisions of a statute, to inflame the minds of the ignorant by appeals to passion, and denunciations of the law as oppressive, unjust, revolting to the conscience, and not binding on the actions of men, to represent the constitution of the land as a compact of iniquity, which it were meritorious to violate or subvert, the mistake has been a grievous one; and they who have fallen into it may rejoice, if peradventure their appeals and their counsels have been hitherto without effect. The supremacy of the constitution, in all its provisions, is at the very basis of our existence as a nation. He, whose conscience, or whose theories of political or individual right, forbid him to support and maintain it in its fullest integrity, may relieve himself from the duties of citizenship, by divesting himself of its rights. But while he remains within our borders, he is to remember, that successfully to instigate treason, is to commit it. I shall not be supposed to imply in these remarks, that I have doubts of the law-abiding character of our people. No one can know them well, without the most entire reliance on their fidelity to the constitution. Some of them may differ from the mass, as to the rightfulness or the wisdom of this or the other provision that is found in the federal compact, they may be divided in sentiment as to the policy of a particular statute, or of some provision in a statute; but it is their honest purpose to stand by the engagements, all the engagements, which bind them to their brethren of the other States. They have but one country; they recognize no law of higher social obligation than its constitution and the laws made in pursuance of it; they recognize no higher appeal than to the tribunals it has appointed; they cherish no patriotism that looks beyond the union of the States. That there are men here, as elsewhere, whom a misguided zeal impels to violations of law; that there are others who are controlled by false sympathies, and some who yield too readily and too fully to sympathies not always false, or if false, yet pardonable, and become criminal by yielding, that we have, not only in our jails and almshouses, but segregated here and there in detached portions of the State, ignorant men, many of them without political rights, degraded in social position, and instinctive of revolt, all this is true. It is proved by the daily record of our police courts, and by the ineffective labors of those good men among us, who seek to detach want from temptation, passion from violence, and ignorance from crime.

But it should not be supposed that any of these represent the sentiment of Pennsylvania, and it would be to wrong our people sorely, to include them in the same category of personal, social, or political morals. It is declared in the article of the constitution, which I have already cited, that 'no person shall be convicted of treason, unless on the testimony of two witnesses to the same overt act, or on confession in open court.' This and the corresponding language in the act of Congress of the 30th of April, 1790, seem to refer to the proofs on the trial, and not to the preliminary hearing before the committing magistrate, or the proceeding before the grand inquest. There can be no conviction until after arraignment on bill found. The previous action in the case is not a trial, and cannot convict, whatever be the evidence or the number of witnesses. I understand this to have been the opinion entertained by Chief Justice Marshall, 1 Burr's Trial, 195, and though it differs from that expressed by Judge Iredell on the indictment of Fries, (1 Whart. Am. St. Tr. 480), I feel authorized to recommend it to you, as within the terms of the Constitution, and involving no injustice to the accused. I have only to add that treason against the United States, may be committed by any one resident or sojourning within its territory, and under the protection of its laws, whether he be a citizen or an alien. (Fost. C. L. 183, 5.—1 Hale 59, 60, 62. 1 Hawk. ch. 17, § 5, Kel. 38).

Besides the crime of treason, which I have thus noticed, there are offences of minor grades, against the Constitution and the State, some or other of which may be apparently established by the evidence that will come before you. These are embraced in the act of Congress, on the 30th of Sept., 1790, Ch. 9, Sec. 22, on the subject of obstructing or resisting the service of legal process,—the act of the 2d of March, 1831, Chap. 99, Sec. 2, which secures the jurors, witnesses, and officers of our Courts in the fearless, free, and impartial administration of their respective functions,—and the act of the 18th of September, 1850, Ch. 60, which relates more particularly to the rescue, or attempted rescue of a fugitive from labor. These Acts were made the subject of a charge to the Grand Jury of this Court in November last, of which I shall direct a copy to be laid before you; and I do not deem it necessary to repeat their provisions at this time.

Gentlemen of the Grand Jury: You are about to enter upon a most grave and momentous duty. You will be careful in performing it, not to permit your indignation against crime, or your just appreciation of its perilous consequences, to influence your judgment of the guilt of those who may be charged before you with its commission. But you will be careful, also, that no misguided charity shall persuade you to withhold the guilty from the retributions of justice. You will inquire whether an offence has been committed, what was its legal character, and who were the offenders,—and this done, and this only, you will make your presentments according to the evidence and the law. Your inquiries will not be restricted to the conduct of the people belonging to our own State. If in the progress of them, you shall find, that men have been among us, who, under whatever mask of conscience or of peace, have labored to incite others to treasonable violence, and who, after arranging the elements of the mischief, have withdrawn themselves to await the explosion they had contrived, you will feel yourselves bound to present the fact to the Court,—and however distant may be the place in which the offenders may have sought refuge, we give you the pledge of the law, that its far-reaching energies shall be exerted to bring them up for trial,—if guilty, to punishment. The offence of treason is not triable in this Court; but by an act of Congress, passed on the 8th of August, 1845, Chap. 98, it is made lawful for the Grand Jury, empanelled and sworn in the District Court, to take cognizance of all the indictments for crimes against the United States within the jurisdiction of either of the Federal Courts of the District. There being no Grand Jury in attendance at this time in the Circuit Court, to pass upon the accusations I have referred to in the first instance, it has fallen to my lot to assume the responsible office of expounding to you the law in regard to them. I have the satisfaction of knowing, that if the views I have expressed are in any respect erroneous, they must undergo the revision of my learned brother of the Supreme Court, who presides in this Circuit, before they can operate to the serious prejudice of any one; and that if they are doubtful even, provision exists for their re-examination in the highest tribunal of the country."

On the strength of Judge Kane's carefully-drawn up charge the Grand Jury found true bills of indictment against forty of the Christiana offenders, charged with treason. James Jackson, an aged member of the Society of Friends (a Quaker), and a well-known non-resistant abolitionist, was of this number. With his name the blanks were filled up; the same form (with regard to these bills) was employed in the case of each one of the accused. The following is a

COPY OF THE INDICTMENT

Eastern District of Pennsylvania, ss.:

The Grand Inquest of the United States of America, inquiring for the Eastern District of Pennsylvania, on their oaths and affirmations, respectfully do present, that James Jackson, yeoman of the District aforesaid, owing allegiance to the United States of America, wickedly devising and intending the peace and tranquility of said United States, to disturb, and prevent the execution of the laws thereof within the same, to wit, a law of the United States, entitled "An act respecting fugitives from justice and persons escaping from the service of their masters," approved February twelfth, one thousand seven hundred and ninety-three, and also a law of the United States, entitled "An act to amend, and supplementary to, the act entitled, An act respecting fugitives from justice and persons escaping from the service of their masters, approved February the twelfth, one thousand seven hundred and ninety-three," which latter supplementary act was approved September eighteenth, one thousand eight hundred and fifty, on the eleventh day of September, in the year of our Lord, one thousand eight hundred and fifty-one, in the county of Lancaster, in the State of Pennsylvania and District aforesaid, and within the jurisdiction of this Court, wickedly and traitorously did intend to levy war against the United States within the same. And to fulfill and bring to effect the said traitorous intention of him, the said James Jackson, he, the said James Jackson afterward, to wit, on the day and year aforesaid, in the State, District and County aforesaid, and within the jurisdiction of this Court, with a great multitude of persons, whose names, to this Inquest are as yet unknown, to a great number, to wit, to the number of one hundred persons and upwards, armed and arrayed in a warlike manner, that is to say, with guns, swords, and other warlike weapons, as well offensive as defensive, being then and there unlawfully and traitorously assembled, did traitorously assemble and combine against the said United States, and then and there, with force and arms, wickedly and traitorously, and with the wicked and traitorous intention to oppose and prevent, by means of intimidation and violence, the execution of the said laws of the United States within the same, did array and dispose themselves in a warlike and hostile manner against the said United States, and then and there, with force and arms, in pursuance of such their traitorous intention, he, the said James Jackson, with the said persons so as aforesaid, wickedly and traitorously did levy war against the United States.

And further, to fulfill and bring to effect the said traitorous intention of him, the said James Jackson, and in pursuance and in execution of the said wicked and traitorous combination to oppose, resist and prevent the said laws of the United States from being carried into execution, he, the said James Jackson, afterwards, to wit, on the day and year first aforesaid, in the State, District and county aforesaid, and within the jurisdiction aforesaid, with the said persons whose names to this Inquest are as yet unknown, did, wickedly and traitorously assemble against the said United States, with the avowed intention by force of arms and intimidation to prevent the execution of the said laws of the United States within the same; and in pursuance and execution of such their wicked and traitorous combination, he, the said James Jackson, then and there with force and arms, with the said persons to a great number, to wit, the number of one hundred persons and upwards, armed and arrayed in a warlike manner, that is to say, with guns, swords, and other warlike weapons, as well offensive as defensive, being then and there, unlawfully and traitorously assembled, did wickedly, knowingly, and traitorously resist and oppose one Henry H. Kline, an officer, duly appointed by Edward D. Ingraham, Esq., a commissioner, duly appointed by the Circuit Court of the United States, for the said district, in the execution of the duty of the office of the said Kline, he, the said Kline, being appointed by the said Edward Ingraham, Esq., by writing under his hand, to execute warrants and other process issued by him, the said Ingraham, in the performance of his duties as Commissioner, under the said laws of the United States, and then and there, with force and arms, with the said great multitude of persons, so as, aforesaid, unlawfully and traitorously assembled, and armed and arrayed in manner as aforesaid, he, the said, James Jackson, wickedly and traitorously did oppose and resist, and prevent the said Kline, from executing the lawful process to him directed and delivered by the said commissioner against sundry persons, then residents of said county, who had been legally charged before the said commissioner as being persons held to service or labor in the State of Maryland, and owing such service or labor to a certain Edward Gorsuch, under the laws of the said State of Maryland, had escaped therefrom, into the said Eastern district of Pennsylvania; which process, duly issued by the said commissioner, the said Kline then and there had in his possession, and was then and there proceeding to execute, as by law he was bound to do; and so the grand inquest, upon their respective oaths and affirmations aforesaid, do say, that the said James Jackson, in manner aforesaid, as much as in him lay, wickedly and traitorously did prevent, by means of force and intimidation, the execution of the said laws of the United States, in the said State and District. And further, to fulfill and bring to effect, the said traitorous intention of him, the said James Jackson, and in further pursuance, and in the execution of the said wicked and traitorous combination to expose, resist, and prevent the execution of the said laws of the said United States, in the State and District aforesaid, he, the said James Jackson, afterwards, to wit, on the day and year first aforesaid, in the State, county, and district aforesaid, and within the jurisdiction of this court, with the said persons whose names to the grand inquest aforesaid, are as yet unknown, did, wickedly and traitorously assemble against the said United States with the avowed intention, by means of force and intimidation, to prevent the execution of the said laws of the United States in the State and district aforesaid, and in pursuance and execution of such, their wicked and traitorous combination and intention, then and there to the State, district, and county aforesaid, and within the jurisdiction of this court, with force and arms, with a great multitude of persons, to wit, the number of one hundred persons and upwards, armed and arrayed in a warlike manner, that is to say, with guns, swords, and other warlike weapons, as well offensive as defensive, being then and there unlawfully and traitorously assembled, he, the said James Jackson, did, knowingly, and unlawfully assault the said Henry H. Kline, he, the said Kline, being an officer appointed by writing, under the hand of the said Edward D. Ingraham, Esq., a commissioner under said laws, to execute warrants and other process, issued by the said commissioner in the performance of his duties as such; and he, the said James Jackson, did, then and there, traitorously, with force and arms, against the will of the said Kline, liberate and take out of his custody, persons by him before that time arrested, and in his lawful custody, then and there being, by virtue of lawful process against them issued by the said commissioner, they being legally charged with being persons held to service or labor in the State of Maryland, and owing such service or labor to a certain Edward Gorsuch, under the laws of the said State of Maryland, who had escaped therefrom into the said district; and so the grand inquest aforesaid, upon their oaths and affirmations, aforesaid, do say, that he, the said James Jackson, as much as in him lay, did, then and there, in pursuance and in execution of the said wicked and traitorous combination and intention, wickedly and traitorously, by means of force and intimidation, prevent the execution of the said laws of the United States, in the said State and district.

And further to fulfill and bring to effect, the said traitorous intention of him, the said James Jackson, and in pursuance and in execution of the said wicked and traitorous combination to oppose, resist and prevent the said laws of the United States from being carried into execution, he, the said James Jackson, afterwards, to wit, on the day and year first aforesaid, and on divers other days, both before and afterwards in the State and district aforesaid, and within the jurisdiction of this court, with the said persons to this inquest as yet unknown, maliciously and traitorously did meet, conspire, consult, and agree among themselves, further to oppose, resist, and prevent, by means of force and intimidation, the execution of the said laws herein before specified.

And further to fulfill, perfect, and bring to effect the said traitorous intention of him the said James Jackson, and in pursuance and execution of the said wicked and traitorous combination to oppose and resist the said laws of the United States from being carried into execution, in the State and district aforesaid, he, the said James Jackson, together with the other persons whose names are to this inquest as yet unknown, on the day and year first aforesaid, and on divers other days and times, as well before and after, at the district aforesaid, within the jurisdiction of said court, with force and arms, maliciously and traitorously did prepare and compose, and did then and there maliciously and traitorously cause and procure to be prepared and composed, divers books, pamphlets, letters, declarations, resolutions, addresses, papers and writings, and did then and there maliciously and traitorously publish and disperse and cause to be published and dispersed, divers other books and pamphlets, letters, declarations, resolutions, addresses, papers and writings; the said books, pamphlets, letters, declarations, resolutions, addresses, papers and writings, so respectively prepared, composed, published and dispersed, as last aforesaid, containing therein, amongst other things, incitements, encouragements, and exhortations, to move, induce and persuade persons held to service in any of the United States, by the laws thereof, who had escaped into the said district, as well as other persons, citizens of said district, to resist, oppose, and prevent, by violence and intimidation, the execution of the said laws, and also containing therein, instructions and directions how and upon what occasion, the traitorous purposes last aforesaid, should and might be carried into effect, contrary to the form of the act of Congress in such case made and provided, and against the peace and dignity of the United States.

JOHN W. ASHMEAD,
Attorney of the U. S. for the Eastern District of Pennsylvania.

The abolitionists were leaving no stone unturned in order to triumphantly meet the case in Court. During the interim many tokens of kindness and marks of Christian benevolence were extended to the prisoners by their friends and sympathizers; among these none deserve more honorable mention than the noble act of Thomas L. Kane (son of Judge Kane, and now General), in tendering all the prisoners a sumptuous Thanksgiving dinner, consisting of turkey, etc., pound cake, etc., etc. The dinner for the white prisoners, Messrs. Hanaway, Davis, and Scarlett, was served in appropriate style in the room of

Mr. Morrison, one of the keepers. The U. S. Marshal, A. E. Roberts, Esq., several of the keepers, and Mr. Hanes, one of the prison officers, dined with the prisoners as their guests. Mayor Charles Gilpin was also present and accepted an invitation to test the quality of the luxuries, thus significantly indicating that he was not the enemy of Freedom.

Mrs. Martha Hanaway, the wife of the "traitor" of that name, and who had spent most of her time with her husband since his incarceration, served each of the twenty-seven colored "traitors" with a plate of the delicacies, and the supply being greater than the demand, the balance was served to outsiders in other cells on the same corridor.

The pro-slavery party were very indignant over the matter, and the Hon. Mr. Brent thought it incumbent upon him to bring this high handed procedure to the notice of the Court, where he received a few crumbs of sympathy, from the pro-slavery side, of course. But the dinner had been so handsomely arranged, and coming from the source that it did, it had a very telling effect. Long before this, however, Mr. T. L. Kane had given abundant evidence that he approved of the Underground Rail Road, and was a decided opponent of the Fugitive Slave Law; in short, that he believed in freedom for all men, irrespective of race or color.

Castnor Hanaway was first to be tried; over him, therefore, the great contest was to be made. For the defence of this particular case, the abolitionists selected J. M. Read, Thaddeus Stevens, Joseph S. Lewis and Theodore Cuyler, Esqs. On the side of the Fugitive Slave Law, and against the "traitors," were U. S. District Attorney, John W. Ashmead, Hon. James Cooper, James R. Ludlow, Esq., and Robert G. Brent, Attorney General of Maryland. Mr. Brent was allowed to act as "overseer" in conducting matters on the side of the Fugitive Slave Law. On this infamous enactment, combined with a corrupted popular sentiment, the pro-slavery side depended for success. The abolitionists viewed matters in the light of freedom and humanity, and hopefully relied upon the justice of their cause and the power of truth to overcome and swallow up all the Pharaoh's rods of serpents as fast as they might be thrown down.

The prisoners having lain in their cells nearly three months, the time for their trial arrived. Monday morning, November 24th, the contest began. The first three days were occupied in procuring jurors. The pro-slavery side desired none but such as believed in the Fugitive Slave Law and in "Treason" as expounded in the Judge's charge and the finding of the Grand Jury.

The counsel for the "Traitors" carefully weighed the jurors, and when found wanting challenged them; in so doing, they managed to get rid of most all of that special class upon whom the prosecution depended for a conviction. The jury having been sworn in, the battle commenced in good earnest, and continued unabated for nearly two weeks. It is needless to say, that the examinations and arguments would fill volumes, and were of the most deeply interesting nature.

No attempt can here be made to recite the particulars of the trial other than by a mere reference. It was, doubtless, the most important trial that ever took place in this country relative to the Underground Rail Road passengers, and in its results more good was brought out of evil than can easily be estimated. The pro-slavery theories of treason were utterly demolished, and not a particle of room was left the advocates of the peculiar institution to hope, that slave-hunters in future, in quest of fugitives, would be any more safe than Gorsuch. The tide of public sentiment changed—Hanaway, and the other "traitors," began to be looked upon as having been greatly injured, and justly entitled to public sympathy and honor, while confusion of face, disappointment and chagrin were plainly visible throughout the demoralized ranks of the enemy. Hanaway was victorious.

An effort was next made to convict Thompson, one of the colored "traitors." To defend the colored prisoners, the old Abolition Society had retained Thaddeus Stevens, David Paul Brown, William S. Pierce, and Robert P. Kane, Esqs., (son of Judge Kane). Stevens, Brown and Pierce were well-known veterans, defenders of the slave wherever and whenever called upon so to do. In the present case, they were prepared for a gallant stand and a long siege against opposing forces. Likewise, R. P. Kane, Esq., although a young volunteer in the anti-slavery war, brought to the work great zeal, high attainments, large sympathy and true pluck, while, in view of all the circumstances, the committee of arrangements felt very much gratified to have him in their ranks.

By this time, however, the sandy foundations of "overseer" Brent and Co., (on the part of slavery), had been so completely swept away by the Hon. J. M. Read and Co., on the side of freedom, that there was but little chance left to deal heavy blows upon the defeated advocates of the Fugitive Slave Law. Thompson was pronounced "not guilty." The other prisoners, of course, shared the same good luck. The victory was then complete, equally as much so as at Christiana. Underground Rail Road stock arose rapidly, and a feeling of universal rejoicing pervaded the friends of freedom from one end of the country to the other.

Especially were slave-holders taught the wholesome lesson, that the Fugitive Slave Law was no guarantee against "red hot shot," nor the charges of U. S. Judges and the findings of Grand Juries, together with the superior learning of counsel from slave-holding Maryland, any guarantee that "traitors" would be hung. In every respect, the Underground Rail Road made capital by the treason. Slave-holders from Maryland especially were far less disposed to hunt their runaway property than they had hitherto been. The Deputy Marshal likewise considered the business of catching slaves very unsafe.

William and Ellen Craft

FEMALE SLAVE IN MALE ATTIRE, FLEEING AS A PLANTER,
WITH HER HUSBAND AS HER BODY SERVANT

⊂ϝ A quarter of a century ago, William and Ellen Craft were slaves in the State of Georgia. With them, as with thousands of others, the desire to be free was very strong. For this jewel they were willing to make any sacrifice, or to endure any amount of suffering. In this state of mind they commenced planning. After thinking of various ways that might be tried, it occurred to William and Ellen, that one might act the part of master and the other the part of servant.

Ellen being fair enough to pass for white, of necessity would have to be transformed into a young planter for the time being. All that was needed, however, to make this important change was that she should be dressed elegantly in a fashionable suit of male attire, and have her hair cut in the style usually worn by young planters. Her profusion of dark hair offered a fine opportunity for the change. So far this plan looked very tempting. But it occurred to them that Ellen was beardless. After some mature reflection, they came to the conclusion that this difficulty could be very readily obviated by having the face muffled up as though the young planter was suffering badly with the face or toothache; thus they got rid of this trouble. Straightway, upon further reflection, several other very serious difficulties stared them in the face. For instance, in traveling, they knew that they would be under the necessity of stopping repeatedly at hotels, and that the custom of registering would have to be conformed to, unless some very good excuse could be given for not doing so.

Here they again thought much over matters, and wisely concluded that the young man had better assume the attitude of a gentle-

William Craft   Ellen Craft

man very much indisposed. He must have his right arm placed carefully in a sling; that would be a sufficient excuse for not registering,
etc. Then he must be a little lame, with a nice cane in the left hand; he
must have large green spectacles over his eyes, and withal he must be
very hard of hearing and dependent on his faithful servant (as was no
uncommon thing with slave-holders), to look after all his wants.

William was just the man to act this part. To begin with, he was
very "likely-looking;" smart, active and exceedingly attentive to his
young master—indeed he was almost eyes, ears, hands and feet for
him. William knew that this would please the slave-holders. The
young planter would have nothing to do but hold himself subject to
his ailments and put on a bold air of superiority; he was not to deign
to notice anybody. If, while traveling, gentlemen, either politely or
rudely, should venture to scrape acquaintance with the young planter,
in his deafness he was to remain mute; the servant was to explain. In
every instance when this occurred, as it actually did, the servant was
fully equal to the emergency—none dreaming of the disguises in
which the Underground Rail Road passengers were traveling.

They stopped at a first-class hotel in Charleston, where the young
planter and his body servant were treated, as the house was wont to

treat the chivalry. They stopped also at a similar hotel in Richmond, and with like results.

They knew that they must pass through Baltimore, but they did not know the obstacles that they would have to surmount in the Monumental City. They proceeded to the depot in the usual manner, and the servant asked for tickets for his master and self. Of course the master could have a ticket, but "bonds will have to be entered before you can get a ticket," said the ticket master. "It is the rule of this office to require bonds for all negroes applying for tickets to go North, and none but gentlemen of well-known responsibility will be taken," further explained the ticket master.

The servant replied, that he knew "nothing about that"—that he was "simply traveling with his young master to take care of him—he being in a very delicate state of health, so much so, that fears were entertained that he might not be able to hold out to reach Philadelphia, where he was hastening for medical treatment," and ended his reply by saying, "my master can't be detained." Without further parley, the ticket master very obligingly waived the old "rule," and furnished the requisite tickets. The mountain being thus removed, the young planter and his faithful servant were safely in the cars for the city of Brotherly Love.

Scarcely had they arrived on free soil when the rheumatism departed—the right arm was unslung—the toothache was gone—the beardless face was unmuffled—the deaf heard and spoke—the blind saw—and the lame leaped as an hart, and in the presence of a few astonished friends of the slave, the facts of this unparalleled Underground Rail Road feat were fully established by the most unquestionable evidence.

The constant strain and pressure on Ellen's nerves, however, had tried her severely, so much so, that for days afterwards, she was physically very much prostrated, although joy and gladness beamed from her eyes, which bespoke inexpressible delight within.

Never can the writer forget the impression made by their arrival. Even now, after a lapse of nearly a quarter of a century, it is easy to picture them in a private room, surrounded by a few friends—Ellen in her fine suit of black, with her cloak and high-heeled boots, looking, in every respect, like a young gentleman; in an hour after having dropped her male attire, and assumed the habiliments of her sex the feminine only was visible in every line and feature of her structure.

Her husband, William, was thoroughly colored, but was a man of marked natural abilities, of good manners, and full of pluck, and possessed of perceptive faculties very large.

It was necessary, however, in those days, that they should seek a permanent residence, where their freedom would be more secure than in Philadelphia; therefore they were advised to go to headquarters, directly to Boston. There they would be safe, it was supposed, as it had then been about a generation since a fugitive had been taken back from the old Bay State, and through the incessant labors of William Lloyd Garrison, the great pioneer, and his faithful coadjutors, it was conceded that another fugitive slave case could never be tolerated on the free soil of Massachusetts. So to Boston they went.

On arriving, the warm hearts of abolitionists welcomed them heartily, and greeted and cheered them without let or hindrance. They did not pretend to keep their coming a secret, or hide it under a bushel; the story of their escape was heralded broadcast over the country—North and South, and indeed over the civilized world. For two years or more, not the slightest fear was entertained that they were not just as safe in Boston as if they had gone to Canada. But the day the Fugitive Bill passed, even the bravest abolitionist began to fear that a fugitive slave was no longer safe anywhere under the stars and stripes, North or South, and that William and Ellen Craft were liable to be captured at any moment by Georgia slave hunters. Many abolitionists counselled resistance to the death at all hazards. Instead of running to Canada, fugitives generally armed themselves and thus said, "Give me liberty or give me death."

William and Ellen Craft believed that it was their duty, as citizens of Massachusetts, to observe a more legal and civilized mode of conforming to the marriage rite than had been permitted them in slavery, and as Theodore Parker had shown himself a very warm friend of their's, they agreed to have their wedding over again according to the laws of a free State. After performing the ceremony, the renowned and fearless advocate of equal rights (Theodore Parker), presented

William with a revolver and a dirk-knife, counselling him to use them manfully in defence of his wife and himself, if ever an attempt should be made by his owners or anybody else to re-enslave them.

But, notwithstanding all the published declarations made by abolitionists and fugitives, to the effect, that slave-holders and slave-catchers in visiting Massachusetts in pursuit of their runaway property, would be met by just such weapons as Theodore Parker presented William with, to the surprise of all Boston, the owners of William and Ellen actually had the effrontery to attempt their recapture under the Fugitive Slave Law. How it was done, and the results, taken from the *Old Liberator,* (William Lloyd Garrison's organ), we copy as follows:

From the "Liberator," Nov. 1, 1850.
SLAVE-HUNTERS IN BOSTON

Our city, for a week past, has been thrown into a state of intense excitement by the appearance of two prowling villains, named Hughes and Knight, from Macon, Georgia, for the purpose of seizing William and Ellen Craft, under the infernal Fugitive Slave Bill, and carrying them back to the hell of Slavery. Since the day of '76, there has not been such a popular demonstration on the side of human freedom in this region. The humane and patriotic contagion has infected all classes. Scarcely any other subject has been talked about in the streets, or in the social circle. On Thursday, of last week, warrants for the arrest of William and Ellen were issued by Judge Levi Woodbury, but no officer has yet been found ready or bold enough to serve them. In the meantime, the Vigilance Committee, appointed at the Faneuil Hall meeting, has not been idle. Their number has been increased to upwards of a hundred "good men and true," including some thirty or forty members of the bar; and they have been in constant session, devising every legal method to baffle the pursuing bloodhounds, and relieve the city of their hateful presence. On Saturday placards were posted up in all directions, announcing the arrival of these slave-hunters, and describing their persons. On the same day, Hughes and Knight were arrested on the charge of slander against William Craft. The Chronotype says, the damages being laid at $10,000; bail was demanded in the same sum, and was promptly furnished. By whom? is the question. An immense crowd was assembled in front of the Sheriff's office, while the bail matter was being arranged. The reporters were not admitted. It was only known that Watson Freeman, Esq., who once declared his readiness to hang any number of negroes remarkably cheap, came in, saying that the arrest was a shame, all a humbug, the trick of the damned abolitionists, and proclaimed his readiness to stand bail. John H. Pearson was also sent for, and came—the same John H. Pearson, merchant and Southern packet agent, who immortalized himself by sending back, on the 10th of September, 1846, in the bark Niagara, a poor fugitive slave, who came secreted in the brig Ottoman, from New Orleans—being himself judge, jury and executioner, to consign a fellow-being to a life of bondage—in obedience to the law of a slave State, and in violation of the law of his own. This same John H. Pearson, not contented with his previous infamy, was on hand. There is a story that the slave-hunters have been his table-guests also, and whether he bailed them or not, we don't know. What we know is, that soon after Pearson came out from the back room, where he and Knight and the Sheriff had been closeted, the Sheriff said that Knight was bailed—he would not say by whom. Knight being looked after, was not to be found. He had slipped out through a back door, and thus cheated the crowd of the pleasure of greeting him—possibly with that rough and ready affection which Barclay's brewers bestowed upon Haynau. The escape was very fortunate every way. Hughes and Knight have since been twice arrested and put under bonds of $10,000 (making $30,000 in all), charged with a conspiracy to kidnap and abduct William Craft, a peaceable citizen of Massachusetts, etc. Bail was entered by Hamilton Willis, of Willis & Co., 25 State street, and Patrick Riley, U. S. Deputy Marshal.

The following (says the Chronotype) is a *verbatim et literatim* copy of the letter sent by Knight to Craft, to entice him to the U. S. Hotel, in order to kidnap him. It shows, that the school-master owes Knight more "service and labor" than it is possible for Craft to:

BOSTON, Oct. 22, 1850, 11 Oclk P. M.

Wm. Craft—Sir—I have to leave so Eirley in the morning that I cold not call according to promis, so if you want me to carry a letter home with me, you must bring it to the United States Hotel to morrow and leave it in box 44, or come your self to morrow eavening after tea and bring it. let me no if you come your self by sending a note to box 44 U. S. Hotel so that I may know whether to wate after tea or not by the Bearer. If your wife wants to see me you cold bring her with you if you come your self.

JOHN KNIGHT.

P. S. I shall leave for home eirley a Thursday morning.   J. K.

At a meeting of colored people, held in Belknap Street Church, on Friday evening, the following resolutions were unanimously adopted:

Resolved, That God willed us free; man willed us slaves. We will as God wills; God's will be done.

Resolved, That our oft repeated determination to resist oppression is the same now as ever, and we pledge ourselves, at all hazards, to resist unto death any attempt upon our liberties.

Resolved, That as South Carolina seizes and imprisons colored seamen from the North, under the plea that it is to prevent insurrection and rebellion among her colored population, the authorities of this State, and city in particular, be requested to lay hold of, and put in prison, immediately, any and all fugitive slave-hunters who may be found among us, upon the same ground, and for similar reasons.

Spirited addresses, of a most emphatic type, were made by Messrs. Remond, of Salem, Roberts, Nell, and Allen, of Boston, and Davis, of Plymouth. Individuals and highly respectable committees of gentlemen have repeatedly waited upon these Georgia miscreants, to persuade them to make a speedy departure from the city. After promising to do so, and repeatedly falsifying their word, it is said that they left on Wednesday afternoon, in the express train for New York, and thus (says the Chronotype), they have "gone off with their ears full of fleas, to fire the solemn word for the dissolution of the Union!"

Telegraphic intelligence is received, that President Fillmore has announced his determination to sustain the Fugitive Slave Bill, at all

hazards. Let him try! The fugitives, as well as the colored people generally, seem determined to carry out the spirit of the resolutions to
their fullest extent.

ELLEN first received information that the slave-hunters from
Georgia were after her through Mrs. Geo. S. Hilliard, of Boston,
who had been a good friend to her from the day of her arrival from
slavery. How Mrs. Hilliard obtained the information, the impression
it made on Ellen, and where she was secreted, the following extract of
a letter written by Mrs. Hilliard, touching the memorable event, will
be found deeply interesting:

"In regard to William and Ellen Craft, it is true that we received her
at our house when the first warrant under the act of eighteen hundred
and fifty was issued.

Dr. Bowditch called upon us to say, that the warrant must be for
William and Ellen, as they were the only fugitives here known to
have come from Georgia, and the Dr. asked what we could do. I went
to the house of the Rev. F. T. Gray, on Mt. Vernon street, where Ellen
was working with Miss Dean, an upholsteress, a friend of ours, who
had told us she would teach Ellen her trade. I proposed to Ellen to
come and do some work for me, intending not to alarm her. My
manner, which I supposed to be indifferent and calm, *betrayed* me,
and she threw herself into my arms, sobbing and weeping. She, however, recovered her composure as soon as we reached the street, and
was *very firm* ever after.

My husband wished her, by all means, to be brought to our
house, and to remain under his protection, saying: 'I am perfectly
willing to meet the penalty, should she be found here, but will never
give her up.' The penalty, you remember, was six months' imprisonment and a thousand dollars fine. William Craft went, after a time, to
Lewis Hayden. He was at first, as Dr. Bowditch told us, 'barricaded
in his shop on Cambridge street.' I saw him there, and he said, 'Ellen
must not be left at your house.' 'Why? William,' said I, 'do you think
we would give her up?' 'Never,' said he, 'but Mr. Hilliard is not only
our friend, but he is a U. S. Commissioner, and should Ellen be
found in his house, he must resign his office, as well as incur the

penalty of the law, and I will not subject a friend to such a punishment for the sake of our safety.' Was not this noble, when you think how small was the penalty that any one could receive for aiding slaves to escape, compared to the fate which threatened them in case they were captured? William C. made the same objection to having his wife taken to Mr. Ellis Gray Loring's, he also being a friend and a Commissioner."

This deed of humanity and Christian charity is worthy to be commemorated and classed with the act of the good Samaritan, as the same spirit is shown in both cases. Often was Mrs. Hilliard's house an asylum for fugitive slaves.

After the hunters had left the city in dismay, and the storm of excitement had partially subsided, the friends of William and Ellen concluded that they had better seek a country where they would not be in daily fear of slave-catchers, backed by the Government of the United States. They were, therefore, advised to go to Great Britain. Outfits were liberally provided for them, passages procured, and they took their departure for a habitation in a foreign land.

Much might be told concerning the warm reception they met with from the friends of humanity on every hand, during a stay in England of nearly a score of years, but we feel obliged to make the following extract suffice:

EXTRACT OF A LETTER FROM WM. FARMER, ESQ., OF LONDON, TO WM. LLOYD GARRISON, JUNE 26, 1851— "FUGITIVE SLAVES AT THE GREAT EXHIBITION"

Fortunately, we have, at the present moment, in the British Metropolis, some specimens of what were once American "chattels personal," in the persons of William and Ellen Craft, and William W. Brown, and their friends resolved that they should be exhibited under the world's huge glass case, in order that the world might form its opinion of the alleged mental inferiority of the African race, and their fitness or unfitness for freedom. A small party of anti-slavery friends was accordingly formed to accompany the fugitives through the Exhibition.

Mr. and Mrs. Estlin, of Bristol, and a lady friend, Mr. and Mrs. Richard Webb, of Dublin, and a son and daughter, Mr. McDonnell, (a most influential member of the Executive Committee of the National Reform Association—one of our unostentatious, but highly efficient workers for reform in this country, and whose public and private acts, if you were acquainted with, you would feel the same esteem and affection for him as is felt towards him by Mr. Thompson, myself and many others)—these ladies and gentlemen, together with myself, met at Mr. Thompson's house, and, in company with Mrs. Thompson, and Miss Amelia Thompson, the Crafts and Brown, proceeded from thence to the Exhibition. Saturday was selected, as a day upon which the largest number of the aristocracy and wealthy classes attend the Crystal Palace, and the company was, on this occasion, the most distinguished that had been gathered together within its walls since its opening day. Some fifteen thousand, mostly of the upper classes, were there congregated, including the Queen, Prince Albert, and the royal children, the anti-slavery Duchess of Sutherland, (by whom the fugitives were evidently favorably regarded), the Duke of Wellington, the Bishops of Winchester and St. Asaph, a large number of peers, peeresses, members of Parliament, merchants and bankers, and distinguished men from almost all parts of the world, surpassing, in variety of tongue, character and costume, the description of the population of Jerusalem on the day of Pentecost—a season of which it is hoped the Great Exhibition will prove a type, in the copious outpouring of the holy spirit of brotherly union, and the consequent diffusion, throughout the world, of the anti-slavery gospel of good will to all men.

In addition to the American exhibitors, it so happened that the American visitors were particularly numerous, among whom the experienced eyes of Brown and the Crafts enabled them to detect slaveholders by dozens. Mr. McDonnell escorted Mrs. Craft, and Mrs. Thompson; Miss Thompson, at her own request, took the arm of Wm. Wells Brown, whose companion she elected to be for the day; Wm. Craft walked with Miss Amelia Thompson and myself. This arrangement was purposely made in order that there might be no appearance of patronizing the fugitives, but that it might be shown that we regarded them as our equals, and honored them for their heroic escape from Slavery. Quite contrary to the feeling of ordinary visitors, the American department was our chief attraction. Upon arriving at Powers' Greek Slave, our glorious anti-slavery friend, Punch's 'Virginia Slave' was produced. I hope you have seen this production of our great humorous moralist. It is an admirably-drawn figure of a female slave in chains, with the inscription beneath, 'The Virginia Slave, a companion for Powers' Greek Slave.' The comparison of the two soon drew a small crowd, including several Americans, around and near us. Although they refrained from any audible expressions of feeling, the object of the comparison was evidently understood and keenly felt. It would not have been prudent in us to have challenged, in words, an anti-slavery discussion in the World's Convention; but everything that we could with propriety do was done to induce them to break silence upon the subject. We had no intention, verbally, of taking the initiative in such a discussion; we confined ourselves to speaking at them, in order that they might be led to speak to us; but our efforts were of no avail. The gauntlet, which was unmistakably thrown down by our party, the Americans were too wary to take up. We spoke among each other of the wrongs of Slavery; it was in vain. We discoursed freely upon the iniquity of a professedly Christian Republic holding three millions of its population in cruel and degrading bondage; you might as well have preached to the winds. Wm. Wells Brown took 'Punch's Virginia Slave' and deposited it within the enclosure by the 'Greek Slave,' saying audibly, 'As an American fugitive slave, I place this 'Virginia Slave' by the side of the 'Greek Slave,' as its most fitting companion.' Not a word, or reply, or remonstrance from Yankee or Southerner. We had not, however, proceeded many steps from the place before the 'Virginia Slave' was removed. We returned to the statue, and stood near the American by whom it had been taken up, to give him an opportunity of making any remarks he chose upon the matter. Whatever were his feelings, his policy was to keep his lips closed. If he had felt that the act was wrongful, would he not have appealed to the sense of justice of the British bystanders, who are always ready to resist an insult offered to a foreigner in this country? If it was an insult, why not resent it, as became high-spirited

Americans? But no; the chivalry of the South tamely allowed itself to be plucked by the beard; the garrulity of the North permitted itself to be silenced by three fugitive slaves. . . . We promenaded the Exhibition between six and seven hours, and visited nearly every portion of the vast edifice. Among the thousands whom we met in our perambulations, who dreamed of any impropriety in a gentleman of character and standing, like Mr. McDonnell, walking arm-in-arm with a colored woman; or an elegant and accomplished young lady, like Miss Thompson, (daughter of the Hon. George Thompson, M. C.), becoming the promenading companion of a colored man? Did the English peers or peeresses? Not the most aristocratic among them. Did the representatives of any other country, have their notions of propriety shocked by the matter? None but Americans. To see the arm of a beautiful English young lady passed through that of 'a nigger,' taking ices and other refreshments with him, upon terms of the most perfect equality, certainly was enough to 'rile,' and evidently did 'rile' the slave-holders who beheld it; but there was no help for it. Even the New York Broadway bullies would not have dared to utter a word of insult, much less lift a finger against Wm. Wells Brown, when walking with his fair companion in the World's Exhibition. It was a circumstance not to be forgotten by these Southern Bloodhounds. Probably, for the first time in their lives, they felt themselves thoroughly muzzled; they dared not even to bark, much less bite. Like the meanest curs, they had to sneak through the Crystal Palace, unnoticed and uncared for; while the victims who had been rescued from their jaws, were warmly greeted by visitors from all parts of the country.

Brown and the Crafts have paid several other visits to the Great Exhibition, in one of which, Wm. Craft succeeded in getting some Southerners "out" upon the Fugitive Slave Bill, respecting which a discussion was held between them in the American department. Finding themselves worsted at every point, they were compelled to have recourse to lying, and unblushingly denied that the bill contained the provisions which Craft alleged it did. Craft took care to inform them who and what he was. He told them that there had been too much information upon that measure diffused in England for lying to conceal them. He has subsequently met the same parties, who, with contemptible hypocrisy, treated "the nigger" with great respect. In England the Crafts were highly respected. While under her British Majesty's protection, Ellen became the mother of several children (having had none under the stars and stripes). These they spared no pains in educating for usefulness in the world. Some two years since William and Ellen returned with two of their children to the United States, and after visiting Boston and other places, William concluded to visit Georgia, his old home, with a view of seeing what inducement war had opened up to enterprise, as he had felt a desire to remove his family thither, if encouraged. Indeed he was prepared to purchase a plantation, if he found matters satisfactory. This visit evidently furnished the needed encouragement, judging from the fact that he did purchase a plantation somewhere in the neighborhood of Savannah, and is at present living there with his family.

The portraits of William and Ellen represent them at the present stage of life, (as citizens of the U. S.)—of course they have greatly changed in appearance from what they were when they first fled from Georgia. Obviously the Fugitive Slave Law in its crusade against William and Ellen Craft, reaped no advantages, but on the contrary, liberty was greatly the gainer.

Notes

AMONG MANY ACCOUNTS of the Underground Railroad, we have found the following to be especially useful:

William Still, *The Underground Rail Road* (1872), most easily found in the reprint edition (New York: Arno Press and the *New York Times*, 1968), remains an important work because of its details about fugitives as seen by a free black man who was an officer in the Philadelphia Vigilance Committee.

Levi Coffin, *Reminiscences* (Cincinnati: Western Tract Society, 1876) is a major contribution by the Quaker known as the president of the Underground Railroad. In this extensive account of his abolitionist work, Coffin continually offers a Quaker perspective on his activities.

Wilbur H. Siebert, *The Underground Railroad from Slavery to Freedom* (1898) is available in a reprint (New York: Russell & Russell, 1967). This detailed scholarly study was prepared when many of the conductors on the Underground Railroad were still alive. While much additional information on the Liberty Line has been published in the century since Siebert's book was completed, it is still a major resource and should not be ignored.

Henrietta Buckmaster, *Let My People Go* (1941) has been reprinted (Columbia: University of South Carolina Press, 1992). This carefully researched history of the Underground Railroad adds material not found in Siebert.

William Breyfogle, *Make Free: The Story of the Underground Railroad* (Philadelphia: J. B. Lippincott, 1958) is a gracefully written study for the general audience. Breyfogle includes material not found in Siebert.

Larry Gara, *The Liberty Line: The Legend of the Underground Railroad* (Lexington: University of Kentucky Press, 1967) is a revisionist study. Gara studies the legend of the Underground Railroad and "the elements—facts and fancy—which contributed to its growth." His work deserves careful reading.

William L. Andrews, *To Tell a Free Story: The First Century of Afro-American Autobiography, 1760–1865* (Urbana: University of Illinois Press, 1986) is a basic text. Many of the slaves who published the stories of their lives escaped from bondage on the Underground Railroad. They typically gave little specific information about the conductors on the line in order to protect them. Information about stations on the line was also left vague. The Andrews study is thus of great importance, and the bibliographies are especially useful.

Charles L. Blockson, *The Underground Railroad* (New York: Prentice-Hall, 1987) contains first-person narratives of escapes to freedom—excellent brief selections by fugitives and carefully written headnotes.

Stuart A. Kallen, *Life on the Underground Railroad* (San Diego: Lucent Books, 2000) contains a clear text and many illustrations. Recommended for schools.

Ann Hagedorn, *Beyond the River: The Untold Stories of the Heroes of the Underground Railroad* (New York: Simon & Schuster, 2003) concentrates on the abolitionist activities of the Rev. John Rankin, with much information about the other abolitionists in Ripley, Ohio. This carefully researched book is a major contribution to Underground Railroad studies.

We have used all the books listed above for background information.

Preface

The quotation from John Rankin in the Preface is from Breyfogle, *Make Free*, pp. 67–68.

Introduction

The account in the text of the origin of the term "Underground Railroad" is from Siebert, *The Underground Railroad from Slavery to Freedom*, p. 45. Another version is from Gara, *The Liberty Line*, p. 144n.

The secret codes to indicate that fugitive slaves were being brought to the house of a conductor are from Siebert, *The Underground Railroad from Slavery to Freedom,* pp. 56–57. The note from Putnam is reproduced from p. 57.

Buckmaster in *Let My People Go* discusses the slavery issue in the Colonies, pp. 11–13.

Information about the New England Confederation in 1643 urging no harboring of slaves is from Siebert, *The Underground Railroad from Slavery to Freedom,* p. 19. The quotations from George Washington's letters about escaped slaves are from Siebert, p. 33.

Biographical information about Isaac T. Hopper is from Buckmaster, *Let My People Go,* pp. 27–28.

Charles L. Blockson argues in *The Underground Railroad,* p. 229, that only a small number of Quakers were active abolitionists.

Information about the number of fugitive slaves in Canada is from Gara, *The Liberty Line,* pp. 37–38. Robin W. Winks's *The Blacks in Canada: A History,* 2nd ed. (Montreal and Kingston: McGill-Queen's University Press, 1997) contains inconclusive but useful material on the number of escaped slaves in Canada, pp. 484–496. Speculation on the number of fugitives who were helped in Philadelphia is from Siebert, *The Underground Railroad from Slavery to Freedom,* p. 346. For the reasons slaves fled, see William Still, *The Underground Rail Road,* pp. 1–2.

Information about constitutional issues regarding the return of runaways and the Fugitive Slave Law of 1793 is from Siebert, *The Underground Railroad from Slavery to Freedom,* pp. 20–24.

Biographical information about Thomas Garrett is from Buckmaster, *Let My People Go,* pp. 149–152.

Gara in *The Liberty Line,* p. 36, discusses the number of slaves who excaped.

Information about the bounty on Rankin and other abolitionists is from Siebert, *The Underground Railroad from Slavery to Freedom,* p. 53. For additional information on the bounties offered for Rankin's assassination, see Hagedorn, *Beyond the River,* pp. 2, 143, 215, 260, 286n. Siebert discusses the Fugitive Slave Act of 1850 on p. 23 and elsewhere in his book.

The Thoreau quotation is from *The Norton Anthology of American Literature* (New York: W. W. Norton, 1998), I, 1754.

Siebert in *The Underground Railroad from Slavery to Freedom,* pp. 403–439, lists known Underground Railroad conductors by state. This listing is incomplete (especially for Southern states where conductors had to work in great secrecy) and contains errors, but it does indicate the scope of abolitionist activity state by state. We did a hand count of the lists for Indiana, Ohio, and Pennsylvania, the specific states in which Coffin and Still worked.

For biographical information about Levi Coffin we have used his *Reminiscences* and also Larry Gara, "Levi Coffin," in *American National Biography* (New York: Oxford University Press, 1999) V, 148–149. For placing Coffin in the Quaker tradition, see Ben Richmond's abridged edition of Coffin's *Reminiscences* (Richmond, Ind.: Friends United Press, 1991).

The escape routes Coffin used to send fugitives on to Canada are listed in Siebert, *The Underground Railroad from Slavery to Freedom*, pp. 15–16.

The quotation from Harriet Beecher Stowe's *Uncle Tom's Cabin* describing Eliza's flight over the ice floes on the Ohio River is from the edition edited by Darryl Pinckney (New York: Signet, 1998), pp. 67–68.

For accounts of the Rev. John Rankin's participation in Eliza Harris's escape, see Forrest Wilson, *Crusader in Crinoline: The Life of Harriet Beecher Stowe* (Philadelphia: J. B. Lippincott, 1941), pp. 144–147. Also useful is Paul R. Grim, "The Rev. John Rankin, Early Abolitionist," *Ohio Archaeological and Historical Quarterly* XLVI (July 1937), 140–141. The best discussion is to be found in Hagedorn, *Beyond the River*, pp. 135–139. John P. Parker, the free black man who lived in Ripley, Ohio, devoted a chapter in his autobiography, *His Promised Land*, edited by Stuart Seely Sprague (New York: Norton, 1996), pp. 122–126, to Eliza's story.

John Rankin's account of Eliza Harris's coming to his house is quoted in Breyfogle, *Make Free*, p. 69.

Coffin also wrote about Margaret Garner, who murdered her own daughter to keep the child from being returned to slavery. Coffin's long account is included in this collection. For a more complete study of the Margaret Garner story see Steven Weisenburger's *Modern Medea: A Family Story of Slavery and Child-Murder from the Old South* (New York: Hill and Wang, 1998).

Information about William Still is from Larry Gara's entry on Still in *American National Biography*, XX, 775–776, and from William Loren

Katz's unpaged Introduction to the reprint of Still's *The Underground Rail Road.*

Still's section on Harrison Cary is from *The Underground Rail Road,* pp. 406–408.

Charles L. Blockson in *The Underground Railroad* discusses the Philadelphia Vigilance Committee on p. 234. He discusses the danger of impostors on p. 233. Blockson quotes Still's letter to his daughter about writing a history of the Underground Railroad on p. xi.

Information about Henry Box Brown comes primarily from *Narrative of the Life of Henry Box Brown,* with an introduction by Richard Newman and a foreword by Henry Louis Gates, Jr. (New York: Oxford University Press, 2002). Newman writes about Stearns's defective style on p. xii. Still in *The Underground Rail Road,* p. 81, says Brown did not suffer as much as others. Newman discusses Brown's panorama on p. xxvii and Smith's charges against Brown on p. xxix. He discusses Stephen Foster's "Old Uncle Ned" and quotes it on pp. xxiii–xxv. He quotes Brown's rewrite on pp. xxv–xxvi. Newman on the English edition of Brown's narrative is on p. xii.

Information about the Crafts is from *Running a Thousand Miles for Freedom: The Escape of William and Ellen Craft from Slavery,* with a foreword and biographical essay by R. J. M. Blackett (Baton Rouge: Louisiana State University Press, 1999). The biographical information about the Crafts is from Blackett's biographical essay. Still's comments about William Craft spending much time away from home are on p. 98. Blackett's summary on the importance of the Crafts is on p. 102.

Larry Gara writes about the unique qualities of Still's *The Underground Rail Road* in *American National Biography* XX, 775–776.

Still writes about not romanticizing the events described in *The Underground Rail Road* on p. 5.

Charles L. Blockson writes about distortions in the record of white involvement in the Liberty Line in his *The Underground Railroad,* p. 4.

A NOTE ON THE EDITORS

George Hendrick and Willene Hendrick, independent scholars, live in Urbana, Illinois. Together they have written *The Creole Mutiny: A Tale of Revolt Aboard a Slave Ship* and have edited *Incidents in the Life of a Slave Girl and A True Tale of Slavery,* and *Two Slave Rebellions at Sea.* They have also published *Selected Poems of Carl Sandburg*; Sandburg's *Poems for the People* and *Billy Sunday and Other Poems*; and books on Katherine Anne Porter, Hiram Rutherford, Henry Salt, and Ham Jones.